Bread Upon the Waters

Also by Peter Reinhart

Crust & Crumb
Brother Juniper's Bread Book
Sacramental Magic in a Small Town Cafe

Bread Upon
the Waters

A Pilgrimage Toward
Self-Discovery and
Spiritual Truth

Peter Reinhart

PERSEUS BOOKS
Cambridge, Massachusetts

Many of the designations used by manufacturers and sellers to distinguish their products are claimed as trademarks. Where those designations appear in this book and Perseus Books was aware of a trademark claim, the designations have been printed in initial capital letters.

A CIP catalog record for this book is available from the Library of Congress.

ISBN: 0-7382-0183-9
Copyright © 2000 by Peter Reinhart

Excerpts from an interview with Jacob Needleman and Robert Bly from *Epiphany Journal*, Fall 1984, page 11, reprinted by permission of Epiphany Press.

Perseus Books is a member of the Perseus Books Group

Text design by Heather Hutchison
Set in 11.5-point Centaur by the Perseus Books Group

1 2 3 4 5 6 7 8 9 10—03 02 01 00 99
First printing, December 1999

Perseus Books are available at special discounts for bulk purchases in the U.S. by cor-porations, institutions, and other organizations. For more information, please con-tact the Special Markets Department at HarperCollins Publishers, 10 East 53rd Street, New York, NY 10022, or call 1-212-207-7528.

Find us on the World Wide Web at http://www.perseusbooks.com

Dedication

This book is dedicated to my wife Susan who endured the arduous writing journey with me, and asked the right question that unlocked me at the critical moment: "Do you know how this book is going to end?" It caused a flash of literary zen that revealed not how the book would end, but how it would begin, and the rest took care of itself.

Contents

Acknowledgments		ix
Bread Upon the Waters, an Introduction		xi
1	Awakening	1
2	Stepping into Rebirth	15
3	Embracing the Path	31
4	Acquiring Virtue	49
5	Going Through the Narrow Gate	69
6	Integrating the Inner and Outer Person	91
7	Surrendering to Synergy	109
8	Tempering the Soul	123
9	Living from the Interior Priesthood	141
10	Being in the World but Not of It	165
Afterword		183
Notes		185

Acknowledgments

I want to thank the members of Christ the Saviour Brotherhood, especially Fr. Andrew Rossi and Fr. Herman Podmoshensky for their selfless spiritual vision and direction. Also thanks to Fr. Michael Oyer, a wonderful model of what it means to be a pastor in this most challenging of all ages.

A special thanks to the late Dr. Norman Vincent Peale and his wife Ruth Stafford Peale for their encouragement and good advice to tell lots of stories. And to Dr. James Wyrtzen of the Blanton-Peale Institutes of Religion and Health for organizing a group of fellows for a roundtable that greatly illuminated my research.

Thank you to Dr. Dan Kugler, who revealed much about the realm of pastoral counseling and was helpful in many ways. Also, to Dan Roberts who asked me to take a walk with him at just the perfect moment.

Thank you also to my colleagues at the California Culinary Academy for their daily sacrifices and generosity to the next generation of culinary professionals. Also, to the new generation of "bread revolutionaries" everywhere who have raised the bar of awareness regarding the possibility of world class bread in this country, making the metaphor of this book as timely as it is.

Thanks, as always, to Pam Bernstein, my agent who encouraged me not to give up when I was about to pull the plug.

Heartfelt thanks to Tom Grady, my editor who revealed the principles of writing a readable spiritual book and who evoked from me the fullness of my potential.

Thank you to Evie Richter for a fabulous job of copy editing and catching things that many would have missed.

Finally, a most special thanks to Elizabeth Carduff of Perseus Books, who kept this project alive when others would have abandoned it. She helped me tweak it into final form, and told me when I was in the throes of despair, "I know you can pull this off, you always have before." I could not have finished this book without her support and faith in me.

Introduction

Cast thy bread upon the waters; for thou shalt find it after many days.

Ecclesiastes 11:1

In my bread classes at the culinary academy where I am a full-time baking instructor, a new group of students arrives every five weeks, and I have only those five weeks to teach them everything I know about bread. I begin each new class by stressing two important principles. The first is that their goal as bakers will be to evoke from the wheat the fullness of its potential. This, they will learn, is the baker's craft: the manipulation of time and temperature, the art of fermentation, and mastery of their tools. The second principle is that after they become good at making many types of bread I want them to become excellent at one. I tell my students I want them to first go broad, but then they must go deep.

Many people go through life content with a good but not great standard of expectations. Sometimes this is because they haven't seen a level of excellence that inspires them to dig a little deeper, reach a little higher. For many years the bread scene in the United States was like that, as we settled for mediocre white bread as our standard. In recent years American bakers have broken through to new heights of excellence, even winning the world championship of bread in 1999 in Paris at the Coupe du Monde du Boulangerie. I fully expect my students to tap into that level of excellence within the allotted five weeks, and I know that when they do they will never again view bread, their baking abilities, or themselves the same way. This is because breaking through to true excellence is a type of initiation. It changes you in a way that is tangible and everlasting.

The two principles that I teach in my class are extensions of universal principles that have shaped and changed my life. I did not start out as a bread teacher and never did I think that I would write three books on bread and cooking, becoming a leading spokesman of the emerging bread revolution of the 1980s and '90s. I thought I was headed for a life of Christian ministry, having spent over twenty-five years in seminary training and charitable work as a brother in an Eastern Orthodox service order. Life sometimes takes unforeseen twists and turns, but I've learned that being flexible with those twists and turns is definitely one of the secrets of life.

This book is about those kinds of secrets in our personal, sacred dance with God as life unfolds in its mysterious ways. Many of the principles I learned in my spiritual journey and theological studies have often reappeared in my writings on food, veiled, or garbed in delicious metaphors. The lessons I learned on the streets while working in homeless shelters, group homes, and thrift stores in poor urban neighborhoods serve me well with my current crops of culinary students. My own journey careened so broadly through pathways and tributaries of both the old and new ages that when the paths converged, deepening into an unexpectedly rooted tradition, I realized my most famous bread, Struan, had truly become the symbol of my life.

Struan Micheil is the ancient harvest bread from the isles of western Scotland, originally made only on Michaelmas eve (September 29), in the name of Saint Michael the Archangel. The word *struan* means "the convergence of streams" and is also the name of a Scottish clan. The bread, as far as my wife and I could tell when we went back to Scotland to try to find traces of it, originated on the Isle of Skye in a town called Struanmoor, but it seems nobody makes it there or anywhere in Scotland anymore. It consisted of whatever grains, grasses, and seeds were ready for harvest at the time of the festival, and the loaves were fretted over all night by the women of the house (the mothers and daughters were the designated bakers; fallen loaves meant a year of bad luck). The loaves were then brought to church for an early morning mass where they were blessed by the priest, dedicated to loved ones who'd passed away during the year, and then given out to the poor during a ritual procession through town. My wife, Susan, and I created our own version of this bread, probably much lighter and better than any authentic version, and it put us on the national culinary map in the form of our small, ministry-based restaurant/bakery, Brother Juniper's Café. This business soon grew into a larger bakery, which we eventually sold, allowing us to move back into working directly with people; me as a culinary teacher, writer, and personal career and life coach; and Susan as a nutritional consultant and educator. This current book goes beyond bread, though the image of *struan*, that wonderful Celtic convergence bread from the Isle of Skye will, I'm sure you shall see, continually shine through the pages that follow.

This book is about going both broad and deep. It is about searching, broadcasting seeds, but also about dropping roots. In the following pages, I will be telling you stories from my own life and from the lives of others, sharing my own journey because I think my journey is, to a great degree, your journey. As in my bread classes, there is particular content and information I want to impart, but there is also context. I tell my students that I will give them the information they need to be able to make world-class bread, but it will be useless if they don't bring to the work bench the necessary passion to be a world-class baker. I promise them that if they bring 100 percent of themselves to the bench I will meet them with equal intensity, and then all sorts of magic can happen.

Passion for self-knowledge is a necessary prerequisite if the information that follows is to be of any value. There are things that worked for me in my search for meaning, and there are discoveries I made of life's principles that will also work for you as you seek deeper levels of meaningfulness in your life. Passion for the search is the necessary context; the content will follow and be useful only in that context.

Permit me one final bread analogy before I cast it all on the waters and let it float us downstream. There are twelve stages of bread production:

mise en place (gathering and measuring the ingredients);
mixing;
primary fermentation;
punching down the dough (also called degassing);
weighing the individual pieces of dough;
rounding them;
resting them (also called benching);
shaping them into loaves;
secondary fermentation (called proofing);
baking;
cooling;
eating or storing.

Within these twelve stages, which form the framework of all breads, there are actions and principles at work. The most important is fermentation of the grain and dough, which is based on the manipulation of time and temperature. Long, slow fermentation brings forth better-tasting bread, allowing the complex but taste-less starch molecules to gently unwind, splitting off into simpler, but tasty sugar molecules. While this unwinding and flavor development is occurring, life goes on for the baker as he or she moves on to other projects, returning to the dough only at the appointed times. Life goes on and all sorts of other, sometimes even unrelated, things happen. Life goes on while the bread, and perhaps also the baker, grows and ferments. A lot can happen while the dough ferments, yet the changes may be so incremental and gradual that we can't see them and don't realize how profound they are until we taste the finished loaf. If everything unfolds just so, and the twelve stages are given the opportunity to patiently fulfill themselves, then we marvel at the results and will never settle for mediocre bread again.

Struan

The term *harvest bread* indicates that there are many ingredients and always more than one kind of grain. The primary grains of Europe, where until the twentieth century Michaelmas was celebrated as one of the major Christian feast days, are wheat, rye, and oats. Most likely, the original struan breads were rather heavy with these grains, and more valued as a symbolic gratitude bread than as a culinary treat. My version, however, eliminates the rye and lightens the loaf so it can be enjoyed as a daily bread—one that children love (Michael is the guardian angel of children). It includes five grains but the dominant one is high-gluten bread flour. The gluten in the wheat flour is the key to a tall, airy loaf, enveloping the other ingredients into its web-like protein structure and providing the elasticity and extensibility for a good expansion.

Mise en Place

Makes I loaf

2 $^1/_2$ *cups high-gluten bread flour* (unbleached, if possible,
    available at most natural food stores and also in
    supermarkets, where it is labeled bread flour)

3 *tablespoons uncooked polenta* (coarse cornmeal)

3 *tablespoons rolled oats* (or instant oats)

3 *tablespoons brown sugar*

2 *tablespoons wheat bran*

I $^1/_4$ *teaspoons salt*

I *tablespoon instant yeast* (or I $^1/_4$ tablespoons active dry yeast
    dissolved in 4 tablespoons warm water)

3 *tablespoons cooked brown rice*

I $^1/_2$ *tablespoons honey*

$^1/_3$ *cup buttermilk* (low-fat or whole milk can be substituted)

Approximately $^3/_4$ *cup water* (room temperature)

I *tablespoon poppy seeds* (for the top)

Mixing

Mix all the dry ingredients, including the salt and yeast, in a
large bowl, stirring to distribute. Add the cooked rice, honey,
and buttermilk, and mix. Then add $^1/_2$ cup of the water, re-
serving the rest for adjustments during kneading. With your
hands squeeze the ingredients together until they make a ball,
adding more water as needed, until all the dry ingredients
have been incorporated into the dough ball. Sprinkle some
flour on the counter and turn the ball out of the bowl and
begin kneading. Add additional water or flour as needed.

Kneading by Hand

It will take about 10 to 15 minutes to knead by hand. The
dough will change before your eyes, lightening in color, be-

coming gradually more elastic and evenly grained. The finished dough should be tacky but not sticky, lightly golden, stretchy and elastic rather than porridge-like. When you push the heels of your hands into the dough, it should give way but not tear. If it flakes or crumbles, add a little more water; if it is sticky, sprinkle in more flour.

Fermentation

Clean out and dry the mixing bowl. Wipe the inside of the bowl with a little oil, or mist with vegetable oil pan spray. Place the dough in the bowl and cover with a damp towel or plastic wrap or place the bowl in a plastic bag. Allow the dough to ferment in a warm place for about 90 minutes, or until it has roughly doubled in size (it may take a shorter or longer time, depending on the temperature).

Forming the Loaf

This recipe makes 1 regular-size loaf of bread (about 1 $1/2$ pounds finished weight). Because the dough is relaxed and supple, and already scaled for one loaf, it can be shaped without first rounding and resting.

Shape the dough into a loaf by pressing it out from the center with the heels of the hands, gently flattening it into a rough rectangle and punching it down, degassing it. Then roll the dough up into a cigar shape and a seam forms. Tuck the end flaps into the seam, and pinch the seam closed with either your fingers or the edge of your hand, sealing it as best you can. Place the loaf, seam side down, in a greased 9" × 4 $1/2$" bread pan. Spray the top with water and sprinkle on the poppy seeds. Cover and allow the dough to proof until it crests over the top of the pan, approximately 90 minutes.

Baking and Cooling

Preheat the oven to 350 degrees (300 degrees if convection). Bake the loaf for approximately 45 to 55 minutes. The loaf should dome nicely and be dark gold. The sides and bottom should be a uniform light golden brown and there should be an audible thwack (or thunk) when you tap the bottom of the loaf. If the loaf is dark on the top but too light or soft on the sides or bottom, return the loaf, not in the pan, to the oven, and finish baking it for a few minutes more, until it is twackable. Bear in mind that the bread will cook much faster once it is removed from the pan, so keep a close eye on it.

Allow the bread to cool on a rack thoroughly, at least 40 minutes, before slicing it.

Eating or Storing

The best way to store bread is to wait until it is completely cooled in the center. This takes about 2 hours. When it is cool, double-wrap the loaf in plastic wrap and either freeze or leave it in a cool place out of the sun. Do not refrigerate it as this dries it out faster. If freezing, it is a good idea to pre-slice the loaf before wrapping so you can pull out only the number of slices needed.

This bread makes the best toast you will ever have and is wonderful with a little melted butter and some jam or jelly. It is also the best bread I have ever had for tuna and chicken salad sandwiches and also for BLTs. There is something almost magical about how the flavor of mayonnaise marries with the light sweetness of this loaf.

———

The journey I'm about to describe is framed around ten stages of spiritual development that parallel the twelve stages of bread production. Each is filled with principles not unlike fermentation:

awakening,
stepping into rebirth,
embracing the path,
acquiring virtue,
going through the narrow gate,
integrating the inner and outer person,
surrendering to synergy,
tempering the soul,
living from the interior priesthood,
being in the world but not of it.

In the pages that follow I will elaborate on these stages, attempting to unwind them as we unwind a starch molecule when bread dough ferments, gradually releasing the simple sugars locked up in the flour. Keep these stages in mind, but remember also that a lot of life takes place during the fermentation process. Slow-rise bread is, as all bakers will tell you, the very best.

1

Awakening

Interstate Highway 80 is a scary road when you have never before been on it, it's your first time west of the Mississippi, and you are only twenty years old, with your thumb out trying to get a ride somewhere south of Jackson Hole, Wyoming. Your hair is long, you are wearing a wool poncho with Aztec designs; your arm is in a sling because you separated your shoulder playing football a few days before; it is 1970, and you have just heard a story about how local cowboys love to cut off the hair of hippies. Interstate 80 may even have the look of a river that leads to General Kurtz, as it disappears in an endless arc over the horizon, shimmering like a desert mirage infected with that unique prairie hybrid of hot dry air and auto exhaust fumes. Meanwhile, four hours have passed and no cars have even hinted at stopping. I was starting to worry.

It was my first on-the-road pilgrimage of self-discovery, though at the time I feared it had become a journey into my own heart of darkness. My imagination was on the verge of going out of control, so I had to decide very quickly whether I was going to be Dean Moriarty, Siddhartha, or a newly created someone in-between. Scanning the possibilities amidst the thumping and clacking but rhythmically repeating sounds of the here-they-come and there-they-go cars and trucks echoing off the highway, I latched onto the mantric notes evoked by that sound and involuntarily began chanting, "Hare Krishna, Hare Krishna, Krishna Krishna, Hare Hare. . . ." I continued this chant for two hours, singing at the top of my lungs since I had no fear of being heard, until a car finally stopped and offered me a ride all the way to San Francisco. I arrived two days later with real flowers in my hair and completed a summer of love and healing in both northern and southern California before returning, a changed person, to my home near Philadelphia.

I had never gotten too involved with the Hare Krishnas, though I twice went to what they called a "love feast" in Boston, where I was a hungry college student looking in my scattergun way for both nutritious food and truth. Believing that the Hare Krishna diet of mainly white rice and white sugar would do me in, and not too fond of the haircuts either, I decided that the way of Krishna the blue avatar was not for me. I did, however, have a hard time getting that song out of my head; it became a tape loop that turned itself on at unexpected times.

When my crosscountry summer adventure ended, returning me to college, I frequently thought back to that time on the highway, chanting my head off while imagining that the words themselves created a cage of protection, projecting a tractor beam to cars still miles away from me and my tired thumb. I thanked God for Krishna and all those bald, pasty-faced Krishnites who infused their song into my heart, replacing my highway fear with highway hope. I have never been quite as chauvinistic about Christianity as I think my Orthodox brethren would like me to be, and I believe those two hours of highway chanting had something to do with it.

What I came to believe is that on Highway 80 my impulsive burst of free-flowing chanting, surrendering to the magic of the road, and abandoning myself to Divine providence was initiatory for me, a crucial step in the unfolding of my soul that eventually, gradually, led me through unanticipated arcs and loops to Eastern Orthodox Christianity. It was a decisive experience, a defining freeze-frame moment, and began a process that was life changing, which is probably as good a definition of initiation as there is. It was the first time that I realized my own life could be, and perhaps would be, as interesting as the lives of my heroes and role models. I can only say this in retrospect, for there was no way to see things in those terms then. It was just one in a series of seemingly random acts I did, only now I don't think of them as random so much as a youthful, unconscious, and serendipity-filled effort to do my part in the ancient synergistic dance between Creator and Creature. I put out the effort and God met me halfway and a process, a long unending process, ensued. In that highway moment I had been given a glimpse, a brief intuitive taste of what I later learned is called in the Judeo-Christian tradition *theosis*, the awareness and experiential knowledge of being created in the image and likeness of God. The glimpse was but an appetizer, a teasing moment of God realization. I had, as I now see it, *awakened*.

3

I used to think that initiations happen only in a certain chronological order. While it may be true that the soul unfolds in a temporally linear fashion, I have learned that it also unfolds in all sorts of nonlinear ways as well. I can pinpoint the defining moments in my life and string them together into an A to Z story, but as my life continues along in its linear reality I find myself also undergoing various permutations, in and out of order, of the ten initiations I'm about to describe. In every moment, it seems, the potential for any one of these or other initiations to occur is ripe, so you may discover what appear to be recurrences and déjà vu as my story unfolds. Please know that it is okay, for instance, to *awaken* time and again, to *be reborn* time and again, and so on, as we become who we are going to be. However, there are some moments that are so definitively defining, so clearly a breakthrough in our soul's unfolding, that we can point to them as truly significant initiations. As they recur in subsequent life situations, appearing now as minor rather than major initiations, a sense of here we go again may set in, but this is a good thing. It's valuable when we can identify the patterns of our lives and know that we are on the right course. That's the whole point of initiations, passing for the first time through gates both broad and narrow, sometimes revisiting them to deepen the learning.

For me the learning began in earnest when I was eighteen and made a very conscious decision to go beyond reading about interesting people and to try to become one. I then fell in love for the first time and shortly thereafter, like so many before me, suffered my first broken heart. I also got a job cleaning stables at one of the top harness racing horse farms in America because I thought I might make a good sulky driver. Within three days I got carried out on a stretcher and nearly died, unable to breathe because I was allergic to horsehair and straw. Then, while working a summer job in the Pocono Mountains of Pennsylvania, I met a guy who thought he was the reincarnation of Jesus Christ. He asked me to be one of his disciples, which I, along with a few other people, pretended to do. A few months later when we all returned either to college or our regular lives, leaving him with no disciples, he killed himself. That sent me, deeply remorseful and depressed, into a search for a meaningful and real spirituality. My friend's suicide had a martyr's effect upon me, eliciting in me a sense of moral obligation for some kind of atonement. Soon, alone and not certain why, I found myself hitchhiking across America. I did not, despite these formative events, believe I was becoming an interesting person. That belief dawned on me later, on Highway 80, as my *mise en place* of collected experiences was beginning to fall into line as I sensed what I was going to make of this life.

4

Mise en place is a French culinary term that means "everything in its place." It is the primary organizational principle in cooking. Before anyone can bake a loaf of bread, for instance, it is necessary to gather the ingredients, properly weigh them, and only then prepare to start. Once the water meets the flour, a process is initiated that does not end until the bread comes out of the oven and is, if it is a worthy loaf, consumed. In culinary academies we teach that the ultimate success of one's dish, whether it be bread, pastry, or hot entrée, is determined during the *mise en place* phase. Some of our instructors chant it again and again like Zen priests with their favorite koan: "*Mise en place* is your friend." *Mise en place* is both the simplest of concepts and the most difficult to teach. Some students never get it: everything in its place *before* you cook; and make sure you have gathered the right ingredients. To do this you have to know what you want to make.

Prior to Highway 80, and well before I ever learned to cook, I lived and gathered my life experiences without knowing what I planned to make of them. I was a film major in college and dropped out because, while discovering I may have had the talent to write and make films, I did not know what I had to say. I wanted to be a film director but had no direction. I even turned down a job working with Otto Preminger, because I was sure that, if I embarked on my film career then, I would be dead or destroyed within a few years.

Like everyone, I had passed through the requisite natural initiations that come simply by growing up, all the standard childhood passages: losing teeth, first kiss, heartache, hobbies, friendships, embarrassments, betrayals, and identity crises. The ingredients were gathered, my *mise en place* was coming together, but I hadn't decided just what kind of loaf I wanted to bake.

Something changed for me when I burst out in chant on Highway 80. I understood myself for the first time as a pilgrim, a spir-

5

itual pilgrim, and realized that in being such a pilgrim my life had acquired direction and purpose. Yet even this took a few years to fully digest. My *awakening* was both an event and an unfolding over time. It was the beginning of a journey that would have many beginnings.

For the past twenty-nine years I have been searching for a deepening of that awakening, the unwinding of the starchy threads of my soul to release their sugary essence. In religious terminology, a moment of awakening or realization is called an *epiphany*, which means manifestation, or the descent of God into the present moment. Others call it an *Aha!* What I experienced convinced me that I'd had a glimpse into the meaning of life, at least of my life, and I did not want to ever be separated from it. I have, since then, often been separated, left only with a memory that fades dream-like into an image, and finally a longing that needs to be constantly renewed lest it fade away altogether.

No single word or group of words can properly describe an epiphany; after all, thousands of books have attempted this impossible task and English is far from the best language in which to attempt describing the indescribable. Sanskrit, Latin, and Greek are all more precise yet even in these ancient languages the task is still impossible. The phrase in English that comes closest, while falling woefully short, is *unconditional love.* In Greek and Latin, however, there are at least four words for such love: *filios* (brotherly), *eros* (attractive, romantic), *caritas* (charitable), and *agape* (dispassionate, Godly, transcendent). The words define love from all sorts of levels and angles, each one capturing only a portion of the experience that *Aha'd* me so many years ago. Since then I have, inevitably, slipped in and out of that awakened state of unconditional love a few times, in and out of that elusive eureka.

A famous mystic, Saint Anthony of Egypt, the founder of Christian desert monasticism, said he experienced the unconditional love of God only five times in his life, spending nearly one hundred years in the wilderness in the attempt to recapture it, each taste feeding his hunger for the next. My goal, ever since Highway 80, in the great and cocky American tradition of which I am proud to be a part, is to experience it constantly. That quest is my mantra—it has given me a sense of mission; it gives thrust and meaning to my life.

In pursuit of that unconditional love, I subsequently have sat at the feet of more than a few eastern gurus, read hundreds of religious and philosophical books, lived in monasteries, placed myself under the direction of spiritual elders, visited the holy land of Eretz Y'Israel, stood at the foot of the hill of Golgotha, and spent thousands of hours in prayer and meditation. My adult life has been an ongoing pilgrimage in search of samadhi, nirvana, illumination, self-realization, theosis, and union with God. Call it what you will, and I have, at times, called it all of these names and discovered that they are not exactly the same. But the one constant in my life is that I have measured every experience against that singular moment of abandonment to Divine providence on Highway 80.

It has not been a fruitless quest. Once, a number of years ago, I reclaimed my *aha!* for a few brief moments while praying in a chapel after a serious bout of despondency. It fortified and carried me, in the spirit of Saint Anthony, into the next phase of my search, back into the desert. At times my toes have touched the brink of that elusive river, and other times despair caused me to forget what force was driving me, or dashed any hope that it was reattainable, or that it had ever been attained at all. I have, in other words, been alive and fully human—but not always consciously, not always vibrantly, despite my best efforts to maintain the pilgrim's edge and the magic of the road.

In the course of this quest I have made many notes and have had my share of major and minor insights, discovering that part of the process of my personal journey is communicating with others. Every adventure that I pursue always seems to include this aspect, even in the simple baking and writing about a loaf of bread. If my vocation is *spiritual pilgrim*, then my avocation is not baker, but rather, *communicator.*

I learned that the best way to reflect on the meaning and purpose of life is allegorically, metaphorically, and analogously; the images I have to reflect upon are the ones that appeared in my life, most notably bread, which has become my sled dog. I am not anyone's guru or spiritual father but offer the thoughts that follow as much for my own sake as for others. I am convinced that in every moment, as I work out my own destiny, communicating and effectively touching lives is essential to that process. I am still searching for those five epiphanies of Saint Anthony, seeking the great, eternal, ongoing, immortal epiphany and, again, in the great American tradition, expect to find it. Once I stepped off Highway 80 and onto the spiritual path the question that then confronted me was, if ultimate meaning is attainable am I willing to pay the price for its acquisition, to follow the breadcrumb trail wherever it leads? That question, like a little lemon shark attached to the back of a blue whale, is always hanging around. I ask it of myself every day, and as I reflect upon it and write about it, am surprised at what I discover.

One of the things I discovered in my own journey is that the psychological answers I sought in my quest for meaningfulness already existed in the traditions that spawned me. My expectation, then, is that if you are a Christian the quest for meaningfulness should make you a more radical one. I expect the same for Jews, Buddhists, Hindus, and Muslims, not because I follow an egalitarian ecumenism in which all paths are equal (I don't, though I once did), but because it takes a radical plunge into a religion's depths to attain the answers we seek to the serious questions of meaningfulness. If you happen to be one of those seekers who is technically unchurched but nevertheless feels an intuitive spirituality, perhaps this book will help you to organize your *mise en place* and discover your next step.

One of my spiritual teachers, recognizing in me a chronic tendency towards comparativeness, encouraged me to "Go deeper, not broader." This has become, as previously mentioned, the guiding principle not only in my life but also in my bread classes. Another man, one of the most brilliant and devout religious scholars I have ever met, is a Sufi (a mystical Muslim). He told me that the only real common ground among religions was to be found by penetrating one's own religion to its most mystical, traditional core, the one leading to union with God. "Perhaps there we might meet. But I only say perhaps."

9

Shortly before he died, the great martial artist, Bruce Lee, developed his own technique of fighting called Jeet Koon Do, based on formless, spontaneous intuitive movements. The few people who had the opportunity to study with him claim that it was the most brilliant form of martial arts ever devised. Lee refused to teach it to anyone unless he had already achieved a black belt or its equivalent in a traditional school of karate, kung fu, tae kwon do, aikido, judo, or jujitso. He said, "I cannot teach you to go beyond form until you have mastered form."

I later discovered that there is a place beyond form in religion as well. It is called spiritual freedom. At some point on our journey, we inevitably encounter those who seem to have found this state of freedom. It is quite inspiring and exhilarating but also very threatening, for an encounter of this nature calls us to dig deeper and get more disciplined. In search of spiritual freedom I quickly learned that without form and structure, in other words without organization, self-discipline, and lots of practice, it cannot be maintained. Spiritual freedom very quickly becomes spiritual self-deception, known to the holy elders of mystical Christianity as *prelest*. That is why *mise en place* is so important as a first step. But there are also necessary intermediate stages of growth that we pass through to connect the moment of spiritual awakening to a mature and integrated realization of our inherent Godliness.

On my personal journey I learned that there existed for me, in the Judeo-Christian tradition, both the tools and a path to God and Self-realization, and a sacred psychology for effective, meaningful living, consistent with my deepest values. The terminology and articulation of this sacred psychology has changed throughout the ages and has taken on sectarian and denominational nuances, but the essence has remained the same.

10   Some modern psychologists and psychiatrists, such as M. Scott Peck, James Hillman, and Thomas Moore (who lived as a monk for twelve years), are beginning to help the public accept the existence of and need for a recovered psychology of the soul. Yet the maps they are drawing, though quite useful, focus primarily on their creative adaptations of Freudian or Jungian models of psychotherapy.

An alternative, in fact a more traditional premise, is based on the root meaning of religion, in Latin *religio*, which means *to be connected to*. We now live in an age where *religio* is an endangered species, made evident by the dichotomies between psychology and religion, religion and everyday life, and everyday life and meaningfulness, playing itself out in our own sense of fragmentation and powerlessness. I still, despite years of training, fight daily against this dichotomy, but now from a new perspective.

We live, I believe, in a critical historical period, during a worldwide spiritual crisis, in which the possibility of *religio* is again upon us. The tools of self-discovery, such as meditation and affirmative prayer, have never been more available and the interest is vast. The soul, if it exists at all, and I am convinced it does, yearns for union, reunion, and communion with its Source, all of which are goals of *religio,* i.e., connectedness. But there is a question of will.

As I became aware of the tools at my disposal in search of a sacred psychology, I also became excruciatingly aware of the many options and choices that needed to be reconciled within me in order to choose wisely. The recovery of sacred psychology, then, became for me also a journey about choosing wisely, and on this journey I learned how the wisdom to choose well, a *transmission of knowledge,* is passed from generation to generation.

My journey in search of *religio* stemmed from a desire for a sacred psychology that could explain to me and properly frame my yearning for meaningfulness. I was also looking for a greater context, a worldview in which both my psychological as well as spiritual and salvational needs would be met. What I discovered and continue to discover in my striving for connectedness, meaningfulness, and unconditional love came to me only after I mixed the ingredients of my *mise en place* into what I at last came to accept as the unfolding of an interesting, maybe even a very interesting, life. I call it my *theostic quest.* But one thing I have learned from others who have followed their quest: We are all interesting; we are all the star of our own story. There comes a time when we awaken to a deeper reality and realize that life has greater meaning in light of that reality. We can choose to pursue it or we can put it off, but, once awakened, we will always know deep in our gut that this greater reality exists. If we get organized, step out, and commit ourselves to the pursuit of truth, to the attainment of our vision, life gets really interesting, and so do we.

11

Mise en Place for Bread Baking

Mise en place means everything in its place, so before making bread, secure these pieces of equipment and tools and ingredients, organize them, and have them standing by, ready to use:

Equipment and Tools

Bread pans or sheet pans

Extra sheet pan or cast-iron skillet to use to create steam for hearth breads

Pizza stone or quarry tiles—called baking stone (optional—you can also bake directly on sheet pans)

Mixing bowls

Sturdy, easy-to-clean counter or work surface for kneading

Electric mixer (optional)

Kitchen scale (optional)

Plastic and metal scrapers

Spatulas (for getting every last drop of liquid ingredients)

Measuring spoons and cups

Baking parchment

Plastic wrap

Sharp bread knife

Sharp razor or razor knife (for scoring or slashing tops of loaves)

Spray bottle for water (for misting the oven to create steam)

Pizza or bread peel (optional, for sliding breads in and out of the oven)

Kitchen towels

Cooking thermometer (probe style, optional but helpful)

Pan spray (optional, but it makes the process easier)

Ingredients

Bread flour (unbleached if possible, high-gluten if available)

All-purpose flour (unbleached, if possible, for better flavor)

Instant, active dry, or fresh yeast (they all work, though in different amounts)

Salt (any type will work, though in different amounts depending upon the coarseness)

Other grains (polenta, wheat bran, rolled oats or oat flakes, rye meal, brown rice, any others that you like as they can often be substituted for one another)

Cornmeal or semolina flour (for dusting under hearth bread loaves)

Milk, buttermilk, or plain yogurt (buttermilk and yogurt give better flavor than regular milk)

Vegetable or olive oil

Specialty ingredients (herbs, spices, seeds such as poppy seeds and sesame seeds and so on)

Sugar (both white and brown)

Honey

Eggs (for Challah and for glazing)

Before beginning the mixing process, measure out all the ingredients to the desired amount. It is much easier to proceed when everything is scaled and ready to go. This is the secret to any success: Get organized, and get everything in its place.

2

Stepping into Rebirth

It is difficult for me to discuss going deeply into the process of spiritual unfoldment without also doing so in the context of bread baking, that's how intertwined they have become for me. In the very first lecture/demo that I give to new students I explain that there are three purposes for mixing bread dough. The first is to distribute the ingredients evenly; the second is to hydrate the ingredients so that the gluten can develop; and the third is to begin the fermentation through hydration of the yeast or leavening. There are other principles of mixing that contribute to great bread, such as mixing only as long as it takes to get the job done, since overmixing can cause oxidation of the flour and perhaps damage to the gluten. An axiom of serious bread bakers is to use only as much yeast as it takes to get the job done. Too much yeast causes the dough to ferment too quickly, which diminishes our ability to evoke the fullest flavors from the grain—it takes time for the starch molecules to unwind into simpler sugars.

There are two kinds of mixing techniques: the direct and indirect methods. The direct method is also called the straight dough method, and the indirect method is sometimes called the sponge or preferment method. It's the preferment method that makes the best bread and has captured the interest of both home and professional bakers of late, because of its ability to evoke the fullest flavor from the grain. This method uses previously fermented bread dough as a preliminary stage towards the mixing of the final dough. The indirect method can be understood as a process of building dough in stages rather than simply mixing it all at one time, adding the earlier aged dough as a time capsule, full of flavor and leavening.

This building method naturally interests me in both literal and metaphorical ways, as it beautifully parallels the initiatory process of the unfolding soul in its advance from *awakening* to *rebirth*, or the process of becoming of a new person. Baptism is the Christian ritual associated with spiritual rebirth, while two prefiguring ritual initiations parallel it in Judaism, circumcision and bar or bat mitzvahs. The internal initiatory experience, or life-changing moment, does not always correspond simultaneously with the formal external ritual but, in the life of a spiritual pilgrim sooner or later they catch up to each other. Becoming a new person can be, and cannot help but be, a daily event and not just a once-in-a-lifetime experience, so I want to reiterate that minor initiations often occur, as if reinforcements of the initiatory breakthrough or defining moment.

I began building my newly awakened life in earnest the night I saw Richard Alpert at his first public appearance in his new persona as Baba Ram Dass in 1970. He had just returned from India, renounced LSD, and talked of love and the transformation of his life through discipleship to a guru he simply called Baba. Hundreds of us gathered at the Arlington Street Church in downtown Boston, alerted only through the grapevine that Timothy Leary's Harvard buddy was back from India, giving a talk, and the word on the streets was, "Don't miss it."

Alpert, now Ram Dass, was a great storyteller, with the style and engaging cadences of a barefoot rabbi, but in a long, flowing saffron robe, with the smell of incense around him, and a fabulous, envy-inducing beard that he twirled and played with all evening long when he wasn't giving himself foot massages. He was a master of long pauses, closing his eyes to look inward before speaking, making sure his words were just so as he announced it was time for serious God seekers to take the next step. He was the perfect personality at just the right time, and I was mesmerized. At the end of the evening I signed a guest book and was promised a package in the mail. A few months later, I announced to all my friends that I was dropping out of college to drive out to California in the school bus a friend and I had just bought. We planned to fix it up and take it across the country performing puppet shows and selling *magic herbal elixirs*. Ram Dass's package arrived later that same day. I called a friend who had expressed interest in going to California and invited him and his girlfriend to ride out with me. He said, "We've decided to hold off for a while. We just met some interesting people who are trying to open a vegetarian restaurant on Mass. Ave. and we've decided to help them out. Why don't you come down and meet them, there's something interesting happening here; you might like it."

So I went, grabbing my Ram Dass package to look at while on the streetcar. When I walked into a tiny, walk-down, hole-in-the-wall shop and saw an industrious group of hippies banging away at the walls, stripping paint off of chairs, all enthused about the restaurant they aimed to open in a few weeks, I knew I was never going to do the magic bus trip. I had found my next step. Within minutes everyone was gathered around my Ram Dass package, all abuzz with interest. The package included the first edition, in oversized format, of *Be Here Now* ("an instant classic," we decreed), as well as a phonograph record of Hindu chanting, and lots of pictures and posters of Indian holy men. The book was the perfect bridge between the hippie drug culture and the spiritual seeker movement just hitting full stride. Clever drawings, spiritual concepts phrased in hip jargon, and an earnestness that was powerfully compelling drew us into fellowship together as we read *Be Here Now* to each other.

It took three months to get the restaurant open. During that time we formed a commune, worked during the day, and gathered for family-style meals at night, where we tried out recipes on each other, and did all the things that hippies did back then, including chanting the om every chance we got. When the Root One Café opened in March of 1971 it became a kind of ecumenical hang out for people from many spiritual and dietary paths. During that year I met a succession of very interesting holy men and other assorted characters. I went Sufi dancing with Pir Vilayat Khan, the son of the late great Hazrat Inyat Khan and the successor to his father's mantle. I met Karmu, a black auto mechanic by day and a self-proclaimed shaman by night, who boiled up strange herbal potions and healed people of their ailments by putting them on his lap and shaking them intensely for five minutes, after which he insisted they drink a cup of his nasty-tasting herbal brew. I spent the summer with Maharishi Mahesh Yogi, who brought Transcendental Meditation to the world. Later I switched allegiance to Yogi Bhajan because I really liked the physicality of his Kundalini yoga.

Whenever a holy man or woman came to town, their followers would bring them to our restaurant, where we would feed them in exchange for their words of wisdom and transmission. We met Zen masters, yogis, sikhs, zains, swamis, and kabalistic rabbis. We checked out everyone and everything, sometimes practicing their particular technique and sometimes taking a pass. We were visited by the fourteen-year-old Guru Maharaji, then Kirpal Singh and his Indian rival, Swami Muktananda (brought to us by the now ubiquitous Ram Dass on his next tour through town), who had his own American rival, Swami Rudrananda (called Rudi by those who knew him). I spent Friday evenings with Isabel Hickey, the famous "Christian" astrologer, and her group of eclectic followers, including a carpenter named Mitch (no last name) who looked about as close to what I imagined Jesus must have looked like and who was about the most charismatic person I have ever met. It was a great time to be a seeker, but it was also dawning on many of us that it would soon be time to be a finder.

I learned quite a bit through my brief spiritual flings. It was like taking a crash course in comparative religion, and I grew and gained knowledge from each teacher, and from the various practices they taught. I began to note a common thread in their teachings and also to sense when and why it was time to move on, thankful that there was another path revealed as I grew restless of the one I was doing, engaging as I was in a kind of spiritual promiscuity. My perspective on it now, in retrospect, is that each step was part of an initiatic buildup, necessary passages on my soul's journey that were bringing me closer to my religious destiny, the one I dreaded and avoided, Christianity.

In early 1972 our eclectic group of vegetarian Root One seekers decided to host an ecumenical gathering at our café. The organizers of the gathering invited representatives of every alternative religious movement in the city, a formidable number since Boston was, like San Francisco, quite a mecca for nontraditional groups. Only about ten organizations actually sent representatives to the meeting, but the assembled included Sufis, kabalistic Jews, Buddhists, wiccans, warlocks, macrobiotics, Native Americans, and followers of three different Indian gurus. We shared tea and broke bread together, excited to be on the cutting edge of what we felt was an inevitable tidal wave headed towards worldwide ecumenical peace and harmony. We were, after all, the Woodstock Nation, the Rainbow Generation, and believed passionately in that one universal principle, *unconditional love.*

Somebody suggested we vocalize a mantra together, but that offended some of the others so we dropped the idea, especially when a controversary broke out over whether it should be om or aum. We tried to discuss issues of mutual interest but had difficulty deciding what they might be. A big dispute erupted over whether we should refer to God as He or She, or He/She/It, or Mother/Father/God. About the only thing we did agree on was how good the food tasted and how nice it was to share tea. We finally decided it would be easier to love and support each other by not working together but, instead, getting together from time to time to share a meal, as long as it was not too yin for the macrobiotics. Needless to say, these subsequent get-togethers never came to pass; the world did not need a new tower of Babel.

We were naive and idealistic young seekers on fire to save the world. We may have each had a guru or teacher we followed, but we also, in our glorious egocentrism, believed that we represented a revolutionary generation in the history of the planet, one that had seen the mountain top at an amazingly young age and understood in a new and unique way that there were many paths that converged on this one common peak. We called the peak *unconditional love* but, in actuality, we had no idea what we were talking about. We were aflame with genuine spiritual awakenings but lacked the depth and wisdom that could only be gained from life experience. Without depth we had little basis for a shared spirituality. This gathering, like many a failed casserole from the Root One kitchen, was a learning experience that brought us gradually closer to wisdom, but especially gave new meaning to the phrase *Get real!* It did not, thankfully, dim our enthusiasm for spiritual growth.

In the summer of 1972 the Root One Café commune encountered an unusual growth problem: The yogis amongst us were interfering with the zazen'ers, who were encroaching on the chanters, all of whom were troubled by the unpredictability of the Sufi dancers. It was time, we decided, for a unified spiritual practice. After realizing the futility of a rational dialogue on the matter, and mindful of the failed tea gathering months before, we decided our best hope lay in a common prayer. So we all held hands and prayed for God to send us a path of unification. After closing the prayer meeting with a rousing, resonating om, we let go of the prayer (casting our bread upon the waters!), threw ourselves back into the daily tasks of our restaurant, and waited.

A few weeks later I read that there were esoteric philosophy classes being taught two evenings a week, one block away from our apartment on Putnam Avenue in Cambridge, by a group called the Holy Order of MANS. Ever the pilgrim, I mentioned it to one of my friends and the two of us went over to see what it was like. As we approached the house we noticed a number of young men, dressed in what appeared to be Roman Catholic clergy garb with collars, sitting on the front porch. They welcomed us warmly and explained a little about the class, assuring us that it would be unlike anything we'd ever heard before, and suggesting we set aside any assumptions we might have about Christianity until after the class. We went inside, somewhat dubious about the whole situation. The class was taught by a man they called Master Andrew, who was wearing a white vestment robe. When he entered the room everyone stood up until he invited us to sit. He then taught a class from a book called the *Tree of Life Study Plan*, weaving together a series of concepts that drew upon Eastern religions, Jewish kabalah, and various expressions of mystical Christianity. The entire experience was so unique that I returned two nights later, bringing a large contingent of Root One folk with me, all of them anxious to hear for themselves this interesting hybrid. That night Master Andrew taught a class on the symbolism of the tarot, which really shattered a few concepts we had about Christianity. He explained the kabalistic connections and taught the class as a lesson in esoteric symbolism. We were dutifully impressed. During the next few weeks we continued to attend classes and also the Sunday worship service, which included a communion mass. Participating in Christian church services was about the farthest thing from my intentions. As a form of resistance, and in a vain attempt to retain hold of my free spiritedness, I attended classes and services in the turban I wore when teaching Kundalini yoga classes. Without realizing it then, I was paralleling the preferment method of dough mixing, only I was the preferment, about to be built into a new dough.

In my search for answers to life's big questions I, like so many others, abandoned my own familial religious roots. In addition to learning meditation from Maharishi Mahesh Yogi, various Yoga disciplines from many well-known Hindu and Sikh instructors, Sufi dancing and philosophy from Sufi masters, and Zazen sitting from a well-known Buddhist roshi, I also tested many of the offbeat spin-offs of these. Enlightenment intensives, dietary disciplines that ranged from eating strictly cooked foods to other food systems that demanded eating only raw sprouts, and various massage and other physical therapies were among the many ingredients in my preferment. The problem with all these options, though, is that such a pluralistic buffet gave me spiritual indigestion, and a tendency towards exhibiting the two masters syndrome: *"No man can serve two masters: for either he will hate the one, and love the other; or else he will hold to the one, and despise the other"* (Matthew 6:24). Having shopped around, what I now yearned for was a path to follow completely and single-mindedly. Christianity was a big hurdle for me, though, having been raised Jewish. Jesus Christ represents to a Jew much more threatening implications than Krishna, Buddha, Guru Nanak, or even Mohammed. Yet I was fascinated with the cosmology and methodology offered by this group, the Holy Order of MANS.

During the first few weeks of attending I learned that it had been founded in 1968 in San Francisco by a man named Earl Blighton, who was called Father Paul. He believed that he received a revelation directly from Jesus Christ to begin an order, modeled outwardly on the early Jesuits of Ignatius Loyola but built philosophically on Father Paul's lifetime study of religion. This included both Catholic and Protestant theology, with heavy doses of Masonic and Rosicrucian mysticism, and strong influences from Norman Vincent Peale, Ernest Holmes (author of *The Science of Mind*), and Charles Fillmore (founder of the Unity Church). He developed his own program of spiritual teachings that he called The Tree of Life Study Plan. It included spiritual exercises, Platonic and Neo-Platonic philosophy, Bible study, kabalistic mysticism, scientific prayer, meditation and affirmation, and a strong emphasis on service to the needy. He called his organization a service and teaching order because the primary activity of the members was to perform charitable works and to teach Bible and esoteric philosophy classes to the public. The two most controversial elements of the order were the institution of an ordained priesthood based on Father Paul's personal revelation (as opposed to apostolic succession passed on through the lineage of bishops, as practiced in the Roman Catholic and Orthodox churches), and the teaching of mystical/occult studies such as tarot and astrology, much of it based on earlier writings by people like Paul Foster Case and Manley Palmer Hall.

The Tree of Life Study Plan was a synthesis of many teachings. It included controversial ideas such as reincarnation and methods of applying prayer and visualization to affect healings, but its underlying premises were focused primarily on serving God by serving mankind. The organization, with its Rosicrucian and mystery school influence designed to lead people into experiences of illumination and self-realization, encompassed a hierarchy of leadership that included novices, brothers and sisters, priests (both men and women) and Master Teachers. It was quite attractive to someone like myself, versed in many of these concepts through eastern religions and hungry for a western expression. Most attractive was the conviction of Father Paul that there is such a thing as scientific prayer, i.e., prayer that always gets results. He was offering empowerment!

As part of my youthful seeking, I was fascinated with so-called esoteric philosophy, such as kabalah, tarot, astrology, numerology, even palmistry. One of the things they seemed to have in common was a shared language of universal symbolism. Father Paul, in his Tree of Life Study Plan, emphasized the idea of living symbolism, teaching us to recognize that in each moment everything is a symbol and has significance on many levels. God is speaking to us through them, he taught. "Symbolism is the language of the soul and if one knows the language even a simple circle, square, or triangle can embody many levels of meaning."

Prayer, as Father Paul described it, is a very specific and potent type of symbolism. With it, we were taught, all things are possible and all things are doable. In this sense, The Tree of Life Study Plan was a contemporary expression of ancient esoteric philosophic systems. This was probably the biggest hook that drew people to the Holy Order of MANS in the early days, the sense that prayers could actually make a difference, could affect outcomes. Though not an original idea of Father Paul's, it certainly came in a unique and magnetic package.

Within six weeks of bringing together the Holy Order of MANS and the Root One Café community, we started losing people from our restaurant family; they were joining the order. We spoke with Master Andrew, who advised us that we could form what was called a Christian Community that would allow us to participate in the worship, teachings, and classes of the Order without actually joining the vowed, renunciate body. In essence, we formed a church.

On a bright summer Sunday in August of 1972, having given up all my other spiritual allegiances and practices, I was baptized as a Christian, given the baptismal name Peter (I was Douglas until that moment), and became a founding member of the Christian Community of Boston. Many members of our restaurant commune were still drawn to join the renunciate body of the order, while a few of us remained to keep the Root One going. Soon, the Christian Community of Boston was beginning to draw members not associated with the Root One, from varied backgrounds. Some stayed and some passed through us to the order, and some moved on to other paths.

My life had its own adventures, its own ferment, but a year and a half later, in January, 1974, I joined the Holy Order of MANS as a novice, Brother Peter, and have been a vowed member ever since (though the order itself went through a later rebirth, and me with it). A few months after I joined, the remaining core members of the Root One Café sold the restaurant to a Kundalini yoga group that changed the name to The Golden Temple Conscious Cookery. The Christian Community of Boston, in time, grew to be the largest, healthiest parish community in the entire movement and I reported to St. Petersburg, Florida, to begin my novitiate.

I want to return for a moment to the indirect, or preferment, method of dough mixing. When I teach my students how to make French bread, the most classic of all the great hearth breads, I give them a few recipes to try. French bread consists only of flour, water, salt, and yeast; it is so basic that it is called *pain ordinaire* in France. What is remarkable about it, though, is the many shades of flavor and texture this simple combination can produce. Like cheese, fermented simply from milk and rennet, there are a seemingly infinite number of outcomes that are possible with fermented flour and water.

The baker's art really lies in the fermentation process, and fermentation is initiated during the mixing phase. One of the sample recipes the students use for French bread has enough yeast to ferment the dough in 90 minutes and produce finished loaves within three hours of water hitting flour. We refer to these as serviceable loaves, suitable for emergencies or for making croutons or toasted *crostini* and *bruschette.* They are not acceptable for table service and do not fulfill the goal of making world-class bread. As a result of the rapid fermentation, the crust never attains the proper reddish gold caramelization associated with world-class loaves. The flavors of the wheat, while slightly sweet, especially when a pinch of brown sugar is added to the dough as it so often is in quick recipes, lacks the depth and flavor nuances of loaves from slower-rising dough in which the sweetness is extracted totally from the wheat. A fast-baking loaf is like a young wine full of potential but with its most mysterious and complex flavors still locked up in the tannins, needing time to unwind and release.

One of the most powerful techniques for releasing the flavors trapped in the starchy wheat molecules is to add old dough to the new dough. Prefermented dough, *pâte fermentée*, which is really just day-old fermented French bread dough, increases oven spring by an additional 10 percent, and quantum ages newly mixed dough. *Poolish,* a wet sponge-method developed by Polish bakers and brought to France 150 years ago, has the effect of creating larger holes in the crumb, thus allowing for the release of more complex flavor during the baking cycle. *Biga,* an Italian-style firm preferment, also affects flavor and oven spring in positive ways, adding complexity and instant-aging to new dough.

One of the first principles of education that I uncovered in my training as a culinary teacher is that the process of learning is mainly about taking new knowledge and attaching it to old knowledge. I've built my entire curriculum around that principle, layering lessons upon each other, attaching new pieces of information to ones already in my students' repertoire. Preferments are like old knowledge, adding depth into new, young doughs.

When yeast gets wet and is mixed into the dough, it wakes up and the fermentation process begins, the single-celled yeast fungi feeding off available simple sugars and excreting ethanol alcohol and carbon dioxide as by-products. At the moment this begins the dough is forever changed, transformed from unleavened to leavened bread.

There is a distinct difference between unleavened and leavened dough. Matzoh is unleavened, it has no yeast added to cause it to change. During Passover many Jewish families buy special Kosher for Passover matzoh, made under the strictest supervision. It must be mixed, rolled out, and placed in the oven within eighteen minutes from when the flour meets the water because the rabbinical council that decides such things determined that after eighteen minutes the natural wild yeast living in the flour awakens and begins to ferment the dough. Once dough has been fermented it has, in a sense, passed through its awakening and has been reborn as a new creature, ready to grow and become what it is ultimately going to be.

When I was baptized from Doug to Peter it was not only my named that changed. Everything I had done to that point in my life suddenly became a preferment, old knowledge, that was going to be the foundation for a new round of learning. I did not come to my baptism as unleavened matzoh, of that I am sure. I think my "eighteen minutes" of preleavened existence ended on Highway 80; that was when my yeastiness woke me up and I began the process of growing into *pâte fermentée*, developing and unwinding into something that would be changed again when I became Peter.

Pâte Fermentée
(Prefermented Dough)

This prefermented dough is just like French bread dough but is purposely kept in reserve to improve the final dough of another loaf. It can be made the day before, or kept frozen and pulled out when you get the urge to make French bread. An easy way to have it on hand is to make more dough than you need for the final dough and save a piece of it to be used as *pâte fermentée* for the next batch of dough.

Mise en Place

Makes I ²/₃ pounds *pâte fermentée*

3 ¹/₂ *cups unbleached bread flour* (or all-purpose flour)
I ¹/₂ *teaspoons salt* (2 ¹/₂ teaspoons if using kosher salt)
I *teaspoon instant yeast* (or I ¹/₄ teaspoons active dry yeast dissolved in ¹/₄ cup warm water, or 3 teaspoons crumbled fresh yeast)
I ¹/₄ *cups water* (at room temperature)

Mixing and Primary Fermentation

Combine all the ingredients in a large mixing bowl and stir with a large spoon until they form a ball. Transfer the dough to a floured counter or work surface and knead the dough for about 5 to 7 minutes, or until smooth, elastic, and tacky but not sticky. Add more flour if the dough is too sticky, or more water if it seems too stiff and dry. Clean and lightly oil the mixing bowl, form the dough into a ball and place it in the bowl, turning the dough to coat it with the oil. Cover the bowl with plastic wrap or a damp towel and allow the dough to ferment at room temperature for about 45 minutes. It should be about I ¹/₂ times its original size.

Punching Down and Storing

Punch the dough down and degas it, and shape it again into a ball. Return it to the bowl, cover with plastic wrap, and refrigerate overnight or place in the freezer for later use. The *pâte fermentée* will be usable for up to 3 days if kept chilled in the refrigerator. Kept longer than that it will develop a yeasty, alkaline, alcoholy smell, which is the odor of dead yeast, making it unsuitable for use. However, it will keep for up to 6 months in the freezer if wrapped well in plastic, but remember to pull it out 3 or 4 hours before you need it so that it can thaw at room temperature (or you can also take it out the night before and place it in the refrigerator to thaw more gradually).

29

The great French chef Auguste Escoffier once said that regular cooking is when you take ingredients and do something to them. But great cooking, he said, is when you take ingredients and do something to them—and then you do something else to them. My culinary and spiritual journeys were converging.

3

Embracing the Path

Primary fermentation is the third stage of bread production, and it is the most critical stage in producing world-class bread. All the other stages are necessary and will produce bread, but this is the stage where the flavor and overall quality is determined. Fermentation marks an unalterable and irrevocable change in the dough, fulfilling what was begun in the mixing stage.

The parallel to this in the spiritual journey is the acceptance or embracing of one's path, a mutual event of both choosing and being chosen, of what I referred to earlier as the great synergistic dance. *Synergy*, in its ancient theological definition, means the cooperative action of human efforts meeting the will of God, resulting in an act of unearned grace. As in fermentation, it marks the point of no return, choosing and being chosen, for the moment we embrace the path the path embraces us back.

This embracing was not an instant but an unfolding moment for me. By the time I joined the Holy Order of MANS there were over six hundred members, men and women, some married but mostly single. After passing through my novitiate and student training period, and now confirmed in my new identity as Brother Peter, I became in 1975 a life-vowed member.

During my first-year seminary training in St. Petersburg, I met a popular writer of science fiction and action books. We met at a judo tournament where he was competing as research for a martial arts series he was writing; I was there to pick up one of the kids from our community, the son of our priest, who was earning his first belt. (A unique feature of the Holy Order of MANS was that we had married members, including clergy, many with children.) We struck up a conversation and became friends. The writer was intrigued by the nature of our order and I, a big fan of one of his books, was curious about the process of writing novels. He visited us from time to time and I invited him to come for lunch one day where I served, among other things, some freshly baked bread.

I was the seminary cook, a position that fell to me because the previous cook had been unexpectedly transferred to an assignment better matched to her talents. My three years at Root One paved the way for what turned out to be the most perfect assignment imaginable. The other students worked at outside jobs, bringing in their paychecks to support the center. I had the great good fortune of cooking not only for the students before and after work, but also lunch for our priests and a never-ending stream of guests. It was during my year as cook that I started baking bread, beginning with a simple white bread recipe from the *Joy of Cooking*. (The wonderful irony being that twenty-two years later I was asked to be the editor of the bread chapter for the revised *Joy of Cooking*.)

A few months after visiting us for lunch, as I was preparing for a transfer to our Detroit missionary training center, the writer gave me a carbon copy of his latest science fiction novella. It was about a group of futuristic Christian brothers, members of a benevolent group called the Holy Order of Vision, who chose to stay behind during the final days of breathable air on earth in order to help evacuate the last inhabitants to another planet. The main character was named Brother Paul, but in one scene he was asked by another character, "Where is Brother Peter?" His reply: "He's in the kitchen baking some bread." Not only had I become a character in a book, but also, as I later realized, had my destiny revealed.

I spent the next two years on mission in Detroit, Chicago, and then Raleigh, North Carolina. The vows of the order were poverty, humility, obedience, purity (chastity for the unmarried members), and service. In centers around the country, members lived a life of religious structure: morning devotions and communion at 6:00 A.M., prayers at noon and again at 10:00 P.M. Between the prayer periods members worked either at a regular outside job, earning a paycheck, or in one of our own businesses, which included restaurants, sign making, printing, tailoring, upholstery, and stained glass. Some held positions as administrators at our headquarters, or as house parent/pastors in any of our Brother houses or in the Christian Community churches that grew around the vowed brotherhood. During the evening we studied or taught classes to the public (either Bible or Tree of Life Philosophy classes), or went out on the streets to perform what we called street missions, which consisted of two members going to a particular neighborhood and simply walking around in a prayerful manner, attempting to inconspicuously spread *light and blessing*. If opportunities arose to be of help or to enter into conversation, then so much the better, but the focus was always on service, not conversion. It was our belief, and the order's motto, that *By their fruits ye shall know them.* "Your actions speak so loudly I can't hear a word you're saying," was another way we phrased it. This was an important credo to me because I did not want to be associated with a street-corner evangelistic movement.

One of Father Paul's insights into spiritual dynamics, and the one that probably drew me more than any other to the order, was that the best way to experience God is by serving the God in

33

someone else. (Mother Teresa, one of my later heroes, called it "seeing the face of Jesus in everyone, even the poorest of the poor, the lowest of the low.")

My missionary period included some very valuable character-building experiences. One of my first assignments was running a thrift shop on the north side of Chicago in a Puerto Rican neighborhood. The neighborhood was full of children who enjoyed dropping into the store after school, adopting it as a sort of club-house. With the help of some of the other brothers, the kids and I fixed up the basement into a playroom and held a variety of activities there. Everyday the kids would test me, trying to get away with whatever they could. This included talking back, defiance of the house rules, and even stealing from the store. For a while I tried to New Testament them, by which I mean I was very patient and forgiving, attempting to treat them as if they all knew right from wrong, believing I would eventually convert their behavior with my kindly example. This approach lasted only a few weeks before I realized that the kids thought I was a wimp and would continue to work me over until I gained their respect. These were pretty tough kids, with good hearts but badly in need of discipline.

One day a teenager pushed me too far; he was harassing the goldfish in the thrift store fish tank and would not stop when I asked him. Suddenly, I lost my temper and came down very hard on him, yelling at him at the top of my lungs, my voice coming out deeper, quivering, and more ferocious than I ever imagined possible. It was my first experience of actually getting in someone's face as we stood with noses inches apart while I blasted him. The other kids were stunned watching me go off like that and the boy at the fish tank, one of the tougher, more stubborn of the kids, stared unblinkingly back at me. Finally he said, "Why didn't you say so?" and walked away. His behavior was cooperative for about a week and then we had another go-round, similar in intensity, only this time it was outside the store where the adults could see it. Mothers were hanging out of windows watching and fathers, most of them unemployed and hanging out in small groups on the various corners, turned and observed this intense confrontation. I thought, "Oh boy, I really blew it this time. No one will trust me with their kids anymore." But that is not what happened. Instead, I started getting gifts from some of the mothers and more of the kids came to hang out. During the next few months this confrontational scenario would repeat itself a few more times, though with less frequency between episodes. One of the mothers said to me, "The children love you—you put the fear of God into them."

This was a new concept for me because, though I understood the idea of tough love, I never believed in a fear-based approach to religion. I thought about it for a while and came up with a hypothesis that I called the Old and New Testament Transition Theory. This is it in a nutshell: The Old Testament tells the story of a fearsome God who had to continually deal with, as the Bible puts it, a hard-hearted and hard-headed people, training them during centuries of struggle through a painful purification process, preparing them to be the vehicle for their chosen mission. Until they feared and held Him in awe they did not respect Him, and ended up captive to their enemies many times as part of the learning curve. The New Testament, on the other hand, shifts gears to a story about a redemptive, fatherly God, forgiving and unconditionally loving and benevolent. Without the respect, preparation, devotion, and discipline gained during the preceding centuries, however, the messianic vision could not have been fulfilled.

It is admittedly a simplistic understanding of the Bible, but I was still in the early stages of embracing my path, integrating with it, and putting the pieces of my worldview together. My simplistic theory gave me a paradigm for grasping why these tough children

35

were so responsive to such fiery discipline. This was a very extreme situation and required extreme methods; though looking back now with the luxury of hindsight I see many other ways this discipline could have been instilled more patiently.

The harm in having success with such a method is that I figured it would work everywhere. The following year, when I was a house parent for *undisciplined youths* (that is the technical, politically correct term as well as an apt description) in Raleigh, North Carolina, I tried the same approach and discovered that it was neither appropriate nor effective. It merely reinforced a message of extremism and violence to kids who were deeply psychologically wounded, often by abusive parents. I had to learn ways to transmit discipline other than by this fear-of-God method. While the street kids seemed to thrive on such intensity, other children were too fragile for it to be effective.

In time I learned that there is no quick-fix method in healing wounded souls, and frankly, we are all wounded souls. The Old and New Testament Transition Theory had value for me as an early attempt to map the soul's journey. It served for a while as a template for a type of sacred psychology, but I have learned since then that it requires a lifetime of practice to effectively implement and model a spiritual therapy. The most important lesson I learned, though, is that everyone needs structure and limits. The kids taught me that more effectively than any books possibly could. The lessons I learned from both the Chicago street kids and the Raleigh group-home kids greatly influence my teaching today.

It took me three years to fine-tune the structure of my baking class. I am still finding new ways to build in learning disciplines and weave in lessons from my earlier training. I teach my bread students that the word *leaven* comes from the root word meaning *to enliven, bring to life,* or *vivify.* When I explain to my bread students that primary fermentation is the third stage of dough production,

I am careful to differentiate it from the later stage of secondary fermentation, or proofing. Primary fermentation is also called bulk fermentation. It is the stage in which most of the flavor and character of the dough is determined. With the three purposes of mixing already accomplished, the once lifeless, clay-like substance known as dough is slowly, amazingly vivified. The baker infuses the breath of life, via the yeast, into the inert flour/clay, and a living organism begins to grow. The first fermentation marks the official rebirth of those inert ingredients into the living substance called bread dough.

Lionel Poilane, the most famous bread baker in Paris, told me that he has a policy when hiring apprentice bakers: They must not have worked in other bakeries nor studied in the national baking academies. He says it's just too hard to untrain them of their habits. He prefers novices who are willing to come to him unbaptized, so to speak, to achieve their ferment in his system, to immerse themselves in the Poilane vision of bread baking. Having tasted his bread and visited his *manufactorie* (i.e., *made by hand*) in Bievre, France, I understand the passion he feels in transmitting his knowledge to the next generation of bakers. His method of bread baking requires a tremendous feel for the dough by his bakers. They cannot use thermometers in the oven but must use their hands to determine when the most perfect baking temperature has been achieved in the wood-fired ovens that they have personally stoked. His bakers must take total responsibility from start to finish for the loaves they bake; there are no hand-offs to later shifts. The fermentation of the dough must be accurately timed to assure maximum flavor and leavening. A proper amount of dough must be separated from the batch at just the right moment to be used as preferment for the next round. These are all aspects of the craft, not unlike sensitivities required in other crafts, but especially important because bread is a living, leavened

creature, formed under the watchful eye of the baker who attends
it.

Ed Espe Brown, the author of *The Tassajara Bread Book*, one of the
classics of American baking books, wrote this quote for my first
book: "The baker makes the bread, the making of the bread transforms the baker . . . baking bread is path, sustenance, celebration,
prayer, gift, and gratitude. . . ." When I took my final vows and became Brother Peter, I was transformed into a new person though,
like dough in its first fermentation, I had a great deal of maturing
ahead of me. I was full of both old knowledge and new knowledge and, like a dough going through its series of preferment elab-
orations (bakers call them *builds*) I was broadening my foundation
and at the same time beginning to deepen, to develop character
and, perhaps, flavor.

38

Great French Bread

The use of *pâte fermentée*, or prefermented dough (directions
for making it are on page 39), greatly enhances the flavor,
color, and texture of bread, especially French bread. This
bread, so plain yet so delicious, is simply called *pain ordinaire* in
France. It is the standard by which bread bakers are judged,
because it consists of only a few ingredients and relies totally
on the fermentation skills of the baker to evoke the full flavor potential of the grain. Some bakers use small amounts of
prefermented dough and some use larger quantities. The ultimate results are a combination of the quality of the ingredients and the baker's ability to manipulate time and temperature to draw forth the best possible loaf.

I am always playing with ingredient and technique variations in my search for the perfect loaf. Here is a formula that
makes the best version of French bread I have yet developed,

and it uses a surprisingly large amount of *pâte fermentée.* This is the first method I have found that makes a *boulangerie*-quality loaf, without having to hold the dough overnight in the refrigerator to extend fermentation time.

Mise en Place

Makes several loaves, depending upon shape

1 ²/₃ *pounds pâte fermentée* (full recipe page 28; remove from refrigerator 1 hour before mixing to take off the chill)

3 ¹/₂ *cups unbleached bread or all-purpose flour* (or half bread flour and half all-purpose flour)

1 ¹/₂ *teaspoons salt* (2 ¹/₂ teaspoons if using kosher salt)

³/₄ *teaspoon instant yeast* (or 1 teaspoon active dry yeast dissolved in ¹/₄ cup warm water, or 2 ¹/₄ teaspoons crumbled fresh yeast)

1 ¹/₄ *cups water* (at room temperature)

Mixing and Primary Fermentation

In a large mixing bowl stir together the flour, salt, and yeast (add the instant or fresh yeast directly to the flour; if using active dry yeast, hydrate it first in the warm water, wait 2 minutes, then add it to the flour). Break up the *pâte fermentée* into 6 or 8 smaller pieces and stir them into the flour. Then add the water, stirring everything together until it forms a coarse ball of dough. If the dough seems too stiff or dry, add more water. If it is too sticky, you can adjust this with more flour during the kneading stage.

Turn the dough out onto a lightly floured counter or work surface. Flour your hands and begin kneading the dough, turning and folding it as you press down. The three purposes of mixing are to distribute the ingredients, initiate fermentation, and develop the gluten. The gluten development will take about 10 to 12 minutes of kneading to accomplish. If the dough seems too sticky and slack, sprinkle in more flour as you knead. The finished dough should be tacky but not sticky, meaning that it will adhere to a clean dry finger like a Post-it note, peeling off but not leaving any dough on your finger. When the dough is ready, a small piece of it can be gently stretched and pulled into a paper thin, translucent membrane (this is called the window-pane test). The dough should feel neutral to the touch, neither cold nor warm. It should read between 77 and 81 degrees on an instant-read probe cooking thermometer. If it seems too warm, set it aside to cool down and complete the kneading 15 minutes later (this can happen if you use warm water instead of cool room-temperature water).

When the dough is ready, place it in a lightly oiled bowl, cover with plastic wrap or a damp towel, and allow it to ferment at room temperature for approximately 2 hours, or until doubled in size.

Punching Down, Weighing,
Rounding, Resting, and Shaping

Divide the dough into the desired-size pieces, being careful to degas it as little as possible (removing it from the bowl and dividing it into pieces is enough of a punch-down). A nice *baguette* can be made from a 10-ounce piece of dough. A more plump *bâtard* (torpedo-shaped loaf) can be up to 16 ounces. You can also make a large *boule*-shaped (round ball) loaf up to any size, but typically 1 $^1/_2$ pounds is a good size. There is enough dough to make several loaves, but you might also want to put aside 1 $^2/_3$ pounds to use as *pâte fermentée* another time.

Shape the loaves gently, trying to preserve as much of the gas as possible. To make a *baguette:* Pat the scaled piece of dough into a $3/4$-inch-thick rectangle. Fold the bottom third to the middle and use the edge of your hand to press it into the dough, creating surface tension along the plump bottom. Then fold the top third down to the bottom and again seal it with the edge of you hand or with your thumbs, squeezing out gas only at the seam, but creating a nice surface tension along the skin of the dough. This will make a plump torpedo-shaped loaf (you can stop here to make a *bâtard*, or proceed through the next two steps to complete the *baguette*). Place the torpedo seam side down and cover the dough with a damp towel. Allow it to rest for 10 minutes so the gluten can relax. Then repeat the folding and pressing step above, gently extending the dough to about 12 inches in length by gently rocking and rolling it out from the center as your hands move out towards the ends. Again cover and allow to relax for another 10 to 20 minutes. Repeat the shaping techniques one final time, this time extending the loaf to a length that will fit in your oven on a sheet pan or baking stone. (The larger the oven, the longer you can make the *baguette;* most home ovens can only accommodate an 18-inch-long loaf, but commercial ovens can go up to 24 inches or longer.)

Secondary Fermentation (Proofing)

Transfer the shaped loaves to a sheet pan that has been covered with baking parchment and lightly sprinkled with cornmeal or semolina flour. Cover the loaves with a damp towel or mist with pan spray and cover with a plastic trash bag or plastic wrap. Allow the dough to proof for about 60 to 90 minutes at room temperature, or until the loaves have nearly doubled in size. (You may also slip the pan into a plastic bag, closing it loosely to allow for expansion, and refrigerate the loaves overnight to bake the next day.)

Baking

Preheat the oven to 500 degrees. If using a baking stone, preheat it with the oven, preferably on a middle shelf. While it is heating place an empty sheet pan or a cast iron skillet with an ovenproof handle in the oven to also heat up (this pan can either be above or below the baking shelf). When you are ready to bake, score the loaves with a razor or sharp knife, cutting diagonal slashes about $1/2$ inch deep down the length of the loaf. Short loaves can be slashed once or twice, while longer baguettes can take up to 5 or 6 slashes. Mist the loaves with water and either place the sheet pan in the oven or slide the loaves, parchment and all, directly onto the baking stone. Pour 1 cup of hot water into the hot pan or skillet and close the oven door. After 1 minute, spray the oven with water, hitting the oven walls as well as the bread to create more steam. After 1 more minute repeat this one final time.

Turn the oven down to 450 degrees and continue baking until the loaves attain a rich golden color, approximately 15 to 20 minutes (it will take longer for *bâtards* and *boules*). When the loaves appear to be done, turn off the oven and allow the bread to bake an additional 5 to 10 minutes, removing them only if they appear to be burning. Push them for flavor, extending the baking time to roast the grains as deeply as possible. The longer they bake the crisper the crust will remain. If you chose to hold the shaped loaves overnight in the refrigerator to bake the next day, you will observe a blistering of the finished crust that does not occur on same-day loaves. This adds a dramatic visual quality that many people like.

Cooling and Eating or Storing

When you remove the loaves from the oven, place them on a cooling rack and wait at least 30 minutes before cutting into the bread, as it is still baking while cooling down. To store un-eaten bread, double wrap the completely cooled loaves in plastic wrap and freeze. If you plan to eat the bread within 24 hours, you may also place it in a paper bag to keep the crust crisp, or you can wrap it in plastic wrap, which will soften the crust. This bread can be recrisped by plaing it in a hot oven for 5 minutes. Dry, stale bread (if there's any left, which is un-likely) can be used to make croutons or breadcrumbs.

———————

When I went out on mission and worked as a house parent and counselor for those undisciplined teenagers in Raleigh, it was probably the most challenging job I ever had. Seminary training and Bible study were inadequate tools to prepare me for the in-your-face confrontations of day-to-day youth work. In desperation I began reading every book I could find on counseling techniques and listening skills. I attended seminars and workshops at the University of North Carolina and Duke University and worked closely with professional psychologists and consultants. Suddenly, I found a new admiration for therapists, heightened by an ongoing sense of failure as I felt consistently outmaneuvered by the street-smart intuitiveness of the kids I was supposed to be helping. I soon realized that what I needed was a personal vision and understanding of the soul if I were ever to be an effective counselor. From this training and study I gained a new understanding of the importance of meaningfulness and the healing power of love.

As I studied psychotherapeutic models for healing the soul in their modern, existential articulation, my respect for the Bible and other religions that I had studied took on new depths of appreciation. I realized that a sacred psychology of enormous depth already existed in my religious tradition, but it needed to be tapped and mined in the same way psychologists were integrating Greek myths to support their theories. As I continued my study of the relationship between psychology and religion, I found that many psychologists, most notably Carl Jung and his followers, were trying to build bridges between religion and their science. Before this study I assumed that the psychotherapeutic community held a predisposition towards viewing religion as a psychological/sociological category rather than as a connecting link to a more profound and meaningful reality. I feared that Sigmund Freud spoke for the entire field when he wrote, "Religion is an illusion and it derives its strength from the fact that it falls in with our instinctual desires." My earlier awakening was about breaking free of that view, and I was thrilled to find a possible bridge between the religious and psychotherapeutic worldviews, one that respected the credibility of the religious worldview as a means for the healing of the soul.

I learned that there are essentially three influential psychological paradigms, with their respective patriarchs, for understanding what drives the human psyche: *the will to pleasure* (Sigmund Freud), *the will to power* (Alfred Adler), and *the will to meaning* (Victor Frankl). My leanings were towards the Frankl paradigm. His premise was that a person's search for meaning in life is a primary force, and frustration in this search is often the cause of our anxieties. The solution he proposed was, of course, to reconnect a person with a sense of meaning. This may not clear our lives of problems or obstacles but it enables us to bear the inevitable suffering of life with dignity and purpose. Frankl adopted the existential truism, "He who has a why to live can bear with almost any how."

It is not always the physically strongest who survive inhumane ordeals like concentration camps and gulags, but the ones who seem to find some meaningful purpose in their incarceration. Whether driven by a desire to see a loved one, to preserve sacred rituals and relics, or to survive in order to publish a confiscated manuscript (as in Frankl's survival story), a sense of purpose often means the difference between overcoming or succumbing to illness and/or degradation. Frankl wrote, ". . . what can never be ruled out is the unavoidability of suffering. In accepting the challenge to suffer bravely, life has a meaning up to the last moment, and it retains this meaning literally to the end."

I learned through trial and error that the key to applying the principle of meaningfulness in my work with teenagers was the necessity to love them. "Love is the only way to grasp another human being in the innermost core of his personality" was Frankl's way of saying something that is innate in the Judeo-Christian paradigm. Love is the energy that activates the will, according to both religious and more recent psychological articulations. Even under the most inhumane circumstances, love is a stronger force than despair.

I became convinced that what we consider neuroses and despair over the worthwhileness of life, such as those fears and hurts suffered by the teenagers in my Raleigh group home, is more of a spiritual distress than a mental disease. This insight became very important to me over time as I gradually articulated my own vision and quest for a sacred psychology, in which healing takes place through *religio*, or connecting to meaningfulness.

I suddenly realized, in another of those life-defining aha moments, that the *will to meaning* is a way of describing the driving force of what I call the *theostic* quest, or the yearning for union with God. I first realized it by its absence, in both my Raleigh teenagers and also in the Chicago street kids: the lack of connectedness to meaning. I understood then that the theme of my life, the driving force, was connectedness. It was this realization that led me to view religion in the context of *religio,* and to later explore the concept of an interior priesthood in which we are all, in potential and by birthright, mediators between heaven and earth. I was getting into some deep stuff, starting to form some theories of my own, and wondering where they might lead when stacked up against four thousand years of Judeo-Christian tradition—but it was all there.

A few years later, when I had fulfilled my missionary training and was transferred to our headquarter's seminary in San Francisco, I started a heated discussion by suggesting that the goal of every ordained priest or minister should be to obsolete himself. This was not meant disrespectfully, nor did I, or do I, actually think that this should really ever happen. But I suggested it should be part of a priest's or minister's vision of the job to help all members of the flock realize their own interior priesthood, which is to say, their wholeness, their own integrity as communicants with the Divine. In defending my impudent assertion regarding priests, I noted that the ordination of a priest or minister is a serious matter and not to be minimized. The position itself, I stressed, is a living symbol of spiritual mediatorship and represents the flow of energy from the Creator into creation, the process known as *grace.* A priest and, in some denominations the minister, is ordained to perform sacraments, to celebrate on our behalf special rituals that others are not ordained to perform. Since sacramental rituals are enactments of a spiritual drama in which the energy of God enters the world through the mediation of the priest, who serves as a channel of that grace, I truly value this important and necessary calling. But each of us, in our own way, has the ability to be such channels for grace, even if not as ordained clergy. An important key to our sense of meaningfulness is a sense of this empowerment. Does our existence, can the very fact of our beingness, make a difference in the world? Can we replicate the potency of our Source; can we imitate God in this world? This is what I wanted to know, already believing that the answer was yes. I had come to believe that religion, when practiced as true *religio*, or connectedness, is the bridge connecting us with the source of our existence, our reason for being. In other words, I had come to the conclusion that every human being is, in potential, a *mediator* between heaven and earth. We all have an inner dimension, at the soul level, that could be viewed as an *interior priesthood*.

I had grown during my fermentive training, connecting the breadcrumb trail from my aha! awakening on Highway 80 through the broad-gated Root One years, to the Tree of Life Study Plan, and then into real-life missionary application with troubled teens, to believe that the essence of *religio* is the quest to fulfill the inborn spiritual intuition that whispers to us that we are each connected to the Source of all life. We are born with the means to realize this Source, God, and to become Source-like. I learned years later that in the Orthodox mystical tradition it is called *theosis: directly, personally emanating the energies, or virtues, of God.* It is at this interior level, I decided, that the will to ultimate meaning lies.

Dorothy Sayers, the wonderful writer of both detective mysteries and Christian apologetics, once wrote an essay called *Strong Meat*. She pointed out that Saint Paul made the original distinction between spiritual milk and strong meat in I Corinthians, 3:2. He said, "I have fed you with milk, and not with meat: for hitherto ye were not able to bear it, neither now are ye able." I was realizing, as does every pilgrim at this point of the journey, that it was time to reach for the strong meat and find out if I could handle it, warned by Saint Paul who goes on to say, "But strong meat belongs to them that are of full age, even those who by reason of use have their senses exercised to discern both good and evil" (Hebrews 5:14).

There comes a time in each of our lives when we have to connect the dots of our life experiences and embrace a worldview that
encompasses these dots, which are really the values we hold near
and dear. We may go through this process again and again, but
each time we do it confirms our beliefs of that moment, a freeze
frame of whom we have become. These are defining moments and,
when we look back on the string of such moments it is amazing,
even in our imperfection and incompleteness, to see how perfectly
and completely they lead to the present *now* and to the inevitable
string of outcomes and consequences.

In that particular *now*, I had acquired a vision and a life theme
that became my *will to meaning*. I had attained a *why* to fuel my *how*
and now faced the daunting task of trying to prove it by living it.
Though just a spiritual toddler, I was enlivened by the fire of an
internal fermentation process. I stepped, properly fearful, knowing
that I would be tested and tempered, into the next phase of my
unfolding.

4

Acquiring Virtue

There is a Greek word, *metanoia*, that is used often in Christian mystical theology. It refers to a transformation brought about by repentance. Literally, it means *a change of mind*. There are things we have to do, actions we must take, efforts we must enact if we want the rewards of the spiritual quest, if we want *metanoia*. This effort on our part is our half of the synergistic equation in which God's grace enters our life.

The parallel to this in bread making is the fourth stage, called the *punch down*, because the purpose is to let some of the air out of the dough so it can rise again. Once fermentation begins it is impossible to handle dough without squeezing out some of the air, but in the end it all works to the good, with the secondary rising contributing to the character of the finished loaf.

I really had to come to grips with the build-me-up punch-me-down emotional roller-coaster ride in my missionary work with kids. One of the teenage girls living in our residential program in Raleigh revealed to me that she was practicing to be a witch. She showed me five books she had about witchcraft and personal power, with exercises designed to enhance self-esteem, develop control over others, and create your own destiny. She thought I would be shocked to find her in possession of such anti-Christian material. It was fairly obvious that the girl was having problems with her self-esteem and with peer acceptance and viewed these books as a way to achieve control and power in her life. She took special delight in describing one exercise she called self-fascination:

"You get naked in front of a mirror, light a candle, and look through the flame to the mirror, staring at yourself, into your eyes, looking deeply, searching for the inner person, beyond the eyes, beyond the body. You continually repeat an affirmation like, 'I am beauty incarnate,' or 'My future is in my hands, nobody can prevent me from achieving my heart's desire,' and other similar statements. I love this exercise."

I had been through the counter-culture movement of the 1960s, had seen people overpowered by cocaine addiction, falling in love with Cocamorra, the goddess of the cocaine netherworld. Her exercise was fairly innocent compared to some of the witchcraft I had seen in the streets of Boston during the heyday of street theater and spiritual iconoclasm. I patterned my response after the approach used by Saint Paul on the Areopagus, in the midst of Mars Hill, when he ministered to the Athenians by explaining to them (in Acts 17:19–34) that the unknown God whom they worshipped in their Greek mythos was in fact Jesus Christ.

"I understand what you are studying and realize that it is a kind of magic that you think will help you find your true self," I assured her. "What would you say if I told you there is another magic, far more powerful, yet much safer, and less likely to endanger your soul, that would make those books of yours seem like kindergarten?"

She responded, "Is there really such a thing?"

"Definitely."

"Then, yeah, of course I want to know about it."

I was surprised by her next question. "Do I have to burn my other books in order to be allowed to see it?"

I thought about this for a moment and said, "No. This is what I suggest: Put the witchcraft books under your bed for the next week or two. I'll show you some teachings that I think will impress you beyond what you already know, and then you can decide what to do with the witchcraft books later. I'm not worried about those books."

I gave her some of the lessons from the Tree of Life Study Plan. These dealt with how to use prayer to ask for things within a Christian framework, always asking for God's will to be done to protect against transgressing the fine line between the spiritual and the demonic. These lessons described the power of the sign of the cross as a powerful symbol of protection and affirmation, and of submission to a greater will than our own. She was impressed and began to alter her habits and, over a period of six months, stopped taking drugs, refocused her life, and returned home to live with her parents, who had given up on her thinking she was hopelessly lost. The parents asked me what I had done to reach her. My answer was that I'd found a way to show her that the things she wanted were actually available to her in the Judeo-Christian framework. She was passing through an initiatic period in her life and had made some confusing choices that led to deeper confusion. What she really needed was better road maps, and once she had them she was able to straighten out much of her life without too much additional intervention. To her parents it seemed a miracle; I was also amazed, but it confirmed my confidence in my growing theories regarding the efficacy of a sacred psychology based in yearning for spiritual meaningfulness and empowerment.

I had become alive with an idea, a vision of spiritual empowerment, and was beginning to put the pieces together into a world-

51

view and a strategy for living. Not all my ideas would stand the test of time; I was still a spiritual child feeling my way through the labyrinth of concepts and philosophies of my past. But the broad gate that drew me in was narrowing as I delved deeper into the tradition I had now embraced. What was most important was that I was beginning to correlate the inflow of ideas and experiences into a way of life that was meaningful and filled me with a sense of purpose. Connecting to this vision shored me up over the next few years when inevitable failings and humiliations, the *punch downs,* challenged my tenacity and threatened the air in my newly inflated spiritual balloon.

52

The technical term for the *punch-down* phase of bread production is *degassing.* Both punch down and degassing are apt and evocative, for the fermenting dough needs to have some of its air let out in order to continue to develop. Just as Auguste Escoffier described cooking as the art of taking ingredients and doing something to them—and then doing something else to them—the *punch down* is the something else that allows dough to achieve maturity. Life contains its own natural punch downs; they do not have to be contrived or programmed, but they do test our resolve, tempering us into the hard steel that we must become to carry forth a life mission.

I am often asked how many punch downs, or degassings, can dough endure before it affects the flavor negatively and the dough loses its ability to rise again. The answer is, "It depends." For instance, struan bread, which has a fair amount of sugar and honey and a high percentage of yeast, can only endure one punch down before it is shaped and rises again for its bake. If you try to get a second bulk rise from the dough before shaping the individual loaves, the bread has an alkaline after-taste not unlike the flavor of stale beer. This is because the yeast feeds so quickly on the sugars and creates so much alcohol by-product, it exhausts the food supply for the yeast. The yeast, unable to feed and drugged by the very alcohol it created, starts dying and releasing yet another by-product, glutathiamine, which has an ammonia-like flavor, and also weakens the gluten protein. If you bake this dough, it loses its normally golden color and has that alkaline off-taste.

This doesn't happen with French bread dough because there is very little sugar and yeast in it, allowing the fermentation process to progress much more gradually. The longer fermentation gives the dough, through enzyme activity, the opportunity to release some of the natural sugar locked up in the flour starch, providing a long, slow feeding cycle. This kind of dough not only can endure three to four punch downs, but also tastes better than if baked after only one punch down because more natural sugars are released from within.

The general rule of thumb for degassing dough is that simple breads made with just flour, water, salt, and a small amount of yeast require three or more punch downs to evoke from the grain its fullest flavor. Breads that draw much of their flavor from ingredients like honey, sugar, fat, or dairy often require only one punch down before shaping.

Once you know the dough's ability to tolerate fermentation, leaving enough yeast food in the dough for the final rise before baking (called its *push*), you have acquired important knowledge towards being the creator of great bread. Bread dough, like people, can only tolerate so many punch downs before it goes bad. The bread baker's skill is in knowing just how much fermentation to allow, just how much to stress the process to evoke the finest flavor.

One thing I learned quickly as a newly vowed brother is that taking a vow of humility would bring stress and character building opportunities. In fact, I was learning quite a lot about what living under vows meant. My other vows were service, purity, poverty, and obedience. Each one was like an unceasing prayer transmission, a beseeching to draw unto me the things I'd need to become virtuous. My vows were the pillars of my inner prayer life, the framework around which my character would develop. They were an objectification of my vision and goals for myself, the virtues I sought to personify. As a brother under vows I often experienced myself as the resistant apprentice trying to grow into spiritual adulthood. All of my fiery work with the Chicago street kids was coming back on me, karma-like, to bring about my own humility purification process. Every success or step forward seemed to be accompanied by a corresponding failure or embarrassment as I tested the parameters of my vows. But living in a community of fellow pilgrims, many more earnest and thus further along than I, placed me in a crucible where I could test out my ideas, have them challenged, engage in an ongoing inquiry in search of truth, and learn to not be afraid to make mistakes. In other words, to grow.

Between 1977 and 1981 I lived at our headquarter's seminary in San Francisco; between 1981 and 1987 I lived at the order's retreat center and spiritual headquarters in Forestville, near the Russian River in Sonoma County, about sixty miles north of San Francisco. During those ten years I passed through a number of humility-inducing life lessons. For two years I worked in the financial offices of the order, preparing tax forms and learning basic accounting, while participating in priest training classes for what I anticipated to be an ordained vocation that never materialized. Later, I was put in charge of the publications department of the order and began to write articles for our theological magazine, *Epiphany Journal*. I was then invited to serve on the Board of Directors of the order during which time I was fired from the publications job for mishandling the public relations for an important fund-raising project for Cambodian relief and assigned for two years to be the seminary cook (I could never seem to escape the kitchen). After two years in the kitchen I was then assigned to the Forestville retreat center, where I helped with the organic garden and made sacramental beeswax candles.

During that period I briefly tended the community beehives until I nearly destroyed some of them by improperly trying to combine two small hives into one large hive. I'll never forget the sight. I was following classic beehive protocol in attempting to merge two small colonies by laying one hive's box on top of the other, with a piece of paper blocking their connecting entrances. This was supposed to allow them time to get to know each other while they ate through the paper. It didn't work. Somehow I placed the paper incorrectly and the bees started mingling too soon. Dressed in my stingproof bee suit and bonnet I watched helplessly and in horror as the worker bees went to war. There was nothing I could do; it was as if two genies, each consisting of thousands of vibrating buzzing bundles of energy, were released from their lamps determined to be the only genie left standing at the end of the day. The two camps swarmed around me and their hive boxes, the individual bees smashing into each other like head-butting rams. The air crackled with their impacts as they dropped to the ground stunned or dead. On the top of the boxes the ground troops were engaged in a kind of hand-to-hand combat, the bees wrestling each other down, their small legs furiously scratching out at each other the way cats do when defending their turf. The buzzing sound increased in intensity and then gradually lowered as the number of combatants dwindled. Then I saw one of the queens emerge from the box, pacing powerfully along the frame as if exhorting her troops to victory. Queen-spotting is usually one of the joys of beekeeping during normal tending, as we look through the honeycombed frames to try to find her laying her eggs, clearly a regal presence in a fascinating world. Now this royal queen was in battle frenzy, furious at the disruption of her perfect and orderly world. I was afraid of what she might do to me if she were able to go after the true perpetrator of this disaster. But before she could fix her gaze on me and make her move she was surrounded by enemy soldiers who instinctively knew that putting her down was the key to their victory. They moved in on her as she powerfully flung them off as if she were Toshiro Mifune or Bruce Lee in those samurai and kung fu films. She was bigger and stronger than any two bees and kept the attackers at bay for a few moments, but eventually a number of them jumped her and fought her down, while she vainly tried to rise and inflict as much damage as possible before the inevitable. Three times she rose up, killing a few bees each time, but there were always a few more to jump into their place. I tried to come to her aid, not knowing what I'd actually do if I were able to rescue her, but as I got close and heard the angry buzz of the battle I became too intimidated and unsure of myself to intervene. I had unleashed a process that now had to be played out to its conclusion; these genies could not be put back into their bottles. When the queen at last succumbed to the mob attack, failing to rise yet again, lying there like all the other dead bees, only larger and more stunning in her mortal regality, I forced myself to leave the scene, feeling like the author of death. I went straight to the chapel and prayed tearfully for forgiveness for my clumsiness and failed stewardship. The sound of buzzing, though far up the hill where the battle still raged, seemed to follow me in my inner hearing. I went to the candle shop and felt the beautiful gold altar candles I had made the day before from the wax of other such hives raised for the purpose. We farm these creatures for honey and wax but rarely do any of us get to witness the miracle of the hive, one of the most perfectly organized societies on earth. I had long been appreciative of bees, but now I had become more intimate with them than I imagined possible, as their vengeful god of death, and I mourned.

A few hours later I donned the garb and returned to the hives, discovering thousands of casualties, many of them still locked in rigor-mortis death grips with their enemy cousins. I surveyed the field as a general might after an important battle, walking through the carnage. I was deflated and depleted, feeling as if all virtue were drained from me. Soon thereafter I turned over the beekeeping to another more careful brother. A few days later I returned to the hives to visit the site of my blunder and was astonished to find activity. Apparently the queen of the other hive had survived the war and rallied around her the few survivors from both hives. They did, at last, make their peace and merge under the surviving queen and within a few weeks the hive was thriving, replenished by the birth of the previously laid eggs. Naturally, I felt relieved, but I also felt unalterably changed. The memory of the bee war is still strong with me today, nearly twenty years since the event. The experience had so much sound attached to the pictures, so much feeling attached to the sounds. It entered me on many levels. I believe it humbled me in a profound way as I continued my development at the retreat center.

While engaged in the daily, semi-contemplative activities of gardening, candle making, and property up-keep, I also wrote regularly and served as the designated interviewer for *Epiphany Journal.* I had the opportunity to interview a number of important religious thinkers such as Brother David Stendl-Rast, Henri Nouwen, Raimundo Pannikar, Robert Bly, Jacob Needleman, Frank Schaeffer, and others. In addition, I made cheese twice a week, taught myself how to make hand-crafted paper, traveled as a seminar speaker for the Eleventh Commandment Fellowship, a Christian ecology movement started by our order, and created a number of original herbal sodas and barbecue sauces in my never ending food compulsions. I was also the designated struan baker for the community; and courted my future wife, Sister Susan, who was, naturally, the retreat center cook and with whom, after proposing to her in the walk-in refrigerator, I opened Brother Juniper's Café and Bakery in 1986, sealing the direction of our lives.

To frame this stage of growth, I need to briefly return to the story of the Holy Order of MANS. Shortly after I joined the order in 1975, Father Paul, the founder, died. He was, in time, succeeded by Vincent Rossi, the same person I first knew as Master Andrew in Boston, and whom we now called Father Andrew. By the mid-1970s, the demographics of the order were changing as members married other members and families began to grow. We consolidated membership into a few larger communities, moving away from the small mission houses of three to six people that had been scattered around the country and, by now, into other countries.

Father Andrew, realizing that we had outgrown both the earlier communal models as well as the philosophical teachings of Father Paul, gradually steered the order towards a study of the historical Christian Church, including the works of Saint Thomas Aquinas, Saint Augustine, and other important historical Christian leaders. As we worked our way back to the early, pre-schismatic years of Christendom, this study eventually brought us into contact with the Eastern Orthodox Church, both theoretically and in the personage of Father Herman Podmoshensky, a Russian Orthodox priest/monk, abbot of a monastery in the mountains of northern California. Inspired by the realization that much of what we had studied in the Tree of Life Study Plan existed in a traditional articulation within the mystical theological teachings of historical Christianity, we voted in 1988 to petition for acceptance into the

Eastern Orthodox Church. Father Herman officially joined the order in 1987, and became the abbot of our monasteries, and the *spiritual father* of many of the members. The members were then re-baptised and chrismated (similar to confirmation) and those priests who still felt called to the priesthood were reordained by the Bishop who had accepted us. The name was changed from the Holy Order of MANS to Christ the Saviour Brotherhood, in conformance with Orthodox custom. Christ the Saviour Brotherhood redefined itself as a transjurisdictional Orthodox Christian fellowship. Jurisdictions are the various branches and subbranches of the Eastern Church, such as Greek, Russian, Antiochan, Orthodox Church of America (OCA), etc.

The Holy Order of MANS, as the saying goes, reinvented itself. From a very eclectic, semimonastic sect whose early membership consisted mainly of children of the '60s, we became an Orthodox community of traditional Christians. Along the way many members left, feeling an allegiance to the earlier models or phases that we passed through on our journey to Orthodoxy. Of those who stayed some became true monastics, moving into monasteries under Father Herman or under abbots and abbesses in other jurisdictions. Householders like Susan and I left the communal setting and became financially independent, joining forces with the Christian Community lay members to create parishes. During our first twenty years of existence we had, to a great extent, recapitulated the two thousand-year history of Christendom, exploring the many variations, models, and permutations of ways to be Christian, eventually accepting the oldest, traditional orthodoxy as the most complete expression of our findings.

This sketchy summary of the transformation of the Holy Order of MANS into Christ the Saviour Brotherhood does not fully convey the various studies, evolution, and details of our life but, rather, gives a glimpse of the various currents that helped

form me, converging struan-like into a rather unique loaf. Corre-
lating and synthesizing this traverse has occupied much of my
time and thoughts, drawing from treasure chests of wisdom, old
and new.

During this time of synthesis there was one recurrent theme
that appeared over and over in my attempt to bring the pieces of
my personal quest together: the acquisition of virtue. Sometimes
this search took on deep theological tones, delving into the *theostic*
mystical tradition of the Eastern Church in terms that hold interest only to lifelong theologians; at other times, the striving for
virtue became very mundane and practical, a matter as straightfor-
ward as common courtesy.

60

For example, a few years ago I went to a local coffeehouse for an
early morning meeting with an associate. My hands were filled
with a briefcase and papers, and my mind was wandering towards
the issues we were planning to discuss. As I reached the door of
the cafe another man saw me struggling to open it. He came over
and held the door open so I could enter. I was still preoccupied,
thinking about my meeting, so I simply went in without saying
anything. A few seconds later I heard him say, sarcastically,
"Thank you!" I was deeply embarrassed and weakly replied, "Gee,
I'm sorry—thank you."

It was a little thing but it bothered me all day, causing me to examine my self-centeredness. My thinking ranged from defensive
self-justification ("Why do people need to be thanked—why can't
they just accept courtesy as its own reward?"), to how my actions
fostered another person's cynicism, placing a stumbling block in
his own quest to do good. In the end I actually felt grateful that I
had been called on it, because it woke me up to an important principle that I have tried to enact ever since: the power of courtesy.

Courtesy is, at one level, a type of civility that allows people to
get along better. It also goes deeper than that, an acknowledgment

of someone else's importance and worth. At its most profound level, it recognizes the inherent divinity of another. *The fastest way to know God is to serve the God in someone else* was the compelling teaching that drew me into the spiritual life. The conscious practice of civil courtesies is a way to exercise this teaching.

It took me a while to grasp that being courteous, or being good and doing good things, is not an automatic quid pro quo for spiritual attainment. There are, sadly, plenty of stories of courteous scoundrels, but if we understand the dynamic within true civility it can set a powerful living prayer into motion. Getting along is not an end in itself, but it symbolizes kinship. The practice of courteousness, in its depth, can be internalized and interpreted as a way in which God recognizes God. It is, in that regard, a way of spreading light and virtue. Complex theology and the quest for union with God can, in daily practice, be reduced to such actions. Two simple words, *thank you,* unleash a wave of communion-like energy that connects two passing souls for an instant in a deep and profound way. Basic civility is like the bond that is formed when we share a meal with another. It is a priestly act.

Nowadays, in my work as a bread instructor and also as a mentor/coach, I ask students and clients who are fuzzy about civil values to do an experiment: Try <u>not</u> saying *thank you* or *please* in a situation when you know you should. I also ask them, "What happens when you ask someone to do something for you without saying *please?* What do you feel?" Usually they respond that they feel blocked, incomplete, disconnected. A sense of isolation envelopes them.

These are very simple matters, daily situations, but with vast symbolic and sacred implications. *Please* and *thank you* may be just words, they may even be merely social conventions or customs, but they also, when consciously understood, tap into deep levels of powerful, creative, connective energy.

61

Sacred psychology and the interior priesthood are such deep subjects that it may seem naive to be discussing them in the same breath as common courtesy. Philosophy and theology are certainly more difficult to navigate than lessons in civility. And union with God, *theosis*, the ultimate goal, is a matter so grave and complex that it is scarcely written about at all. But we all need more than concepts and ideas; we need actual practices that make an immediate difference in our lives. I learned during my time in Forestville that the most necessary component in the striving for spiritual meaningfulness is a healthy psyche, and a practical, daily application of our knowledge. I've come to believe that churches, the houses of religion, are first and foremost *hospitals for the soul*, responsible for our spiritual health and the nurturing of our psyches, a function far too rarely undertaken.

I also find it helpful to keep the practice of virtues in the context of its motivation. Much has been written about empowerment practices from the point of view of achieving success in the world, but we need to take the subject deeper, to accomplish success of another order if it is to be deeply meaningful. Both worldly and spiritual success involve empowerment; both involve the quest for meaning, and both partake of the same universal principles. The major difference is the level of consciousness that we bring to the mix. The more conscious we are of spiritual principles, the greater the responsibility we have to conform our actions to that level of knowing.

For example, we can hold a door open for a colleague because it's expected, it makes a good impression, it creates a happier workplace, and it deepens our relationship. These are all good things in themselves. If, however, we understand that holding a door open is a way of imitating the goodness of God, of selfless service, of acknowledging that the other is as godly as we hope we are, of feeding another person's soul a taste of that goodness by creating a channel through which the energy of God can enter the material world, then we have just sacramentalized that action. By so doing we have stepped into the interior priesthood and mediated, even if in a very small way, between heaven and earth. In that very moment we set into motion an action that reflects the highest manifestation of our knowledge of God, and a living prayer bounds through creation, bringing forth whatever fruits it may bear. One action can thus have many different levels of interpretation and empowerment.

In identifying the structures that contribute to a path of sacred psychology, along with all the requisite spiritual practices we each do in conjunction with our various churches, the practice of conscious courtesy and civility is the most powerful, ecumenical, unifying practice at our disposal. The results are both immediate and long-term, especially if the practice is sustained on a regular basis. This is an area of our lives in which we all have immediate control; we do not need a therapist to help us to become civil and courteous, yet, with the exception of severely disturbed individuals, the applied practice of such virtues may contribute more to the formation of a healthy soul than any therapy. When linked to the traditional religious practices of prayer, fasting, and charity (almsgiving), it is possible to understand civility as a tangible manifestation of our spiritual intent.

I once began an observation experiment at the culinary school in San Francisco where I worked. As in any large organization, there is prestige associated with the strata of certain jobs, the "food-chain" we sometimes call it. Naturally, the boss and chief executives rank highest, with the chef/instructors commanding the next caste of perceived importance. Then there are the office workers and administrators, and so on down to the dishwashers and custodial staff. Most of us try not to recognize this pecking order; we want to think of ourselves as egalitarian, but the degree of deference and respectfulness that each category garners reveals the actual order of things. Staff members tend to hang out with people from within their own category, with a little overlap from time to time. I noticed that the lowest rungs on the totem pole, the dishwashers and custodians (also called stewards) often get spoken to in a much more demeaning manner than, say, chef/instructors do. It is common to assume that less educated workers need a more militaristic, impersonal, hardened supervision, and sometimes this approach, valid and justifiable from a certain hierarchical perspective, can tip over into rudeness and disrespect. One rarely hears the words *please* or *thank you* in the chain of command of these workers, except upwardly.

So I decided, along with other of my chef/instructor colleagues, to display courteousness and gratitude to these workers. Every opportunity we could find to offer kindness and appreciation we took. Whenever something got fixed in my classroom or I needed to ask for attention towards a need within the stewards' domain I always made it a point to personally say thank you or to send a note of thanks, or a gift. When walking down the hallway I held the doors open for these workers, engaged them in conversation, and treated them as if their jobs were every bit as important to the success of the school as mine (which they are). As a result, my classroom received exceptional service and there was a constant sense of mutual appreciation and respect between the stewards and maintenance crew and me and my students.

My motives range in degree of purity, and one of my major struggles is with true humility and purity of intent. I've always struggled with the saying of Jesus, "The last shall be first and first last," because when I make myself go last I wonder if I'm doing it merely because I really want to be first. When I attempt to practice the Christian injunction that he who will be greatest is he who serves the most, I grapple with whether I really love serving or am just trying to collect grace chips. What I do know is that I get better with practice and tend not to overthink it as much.

As every priest knows, and ritually reminds himself before taking confessions, no one is truly worthy to be the mediator of grace between heaven and earth, but some are ordained to act so. We all, however, have the power to sacramentalize our daily actions and to raise them to this priestly dimension even though, in our humanity, we are flawed and impure. That is why courtesy is considered a graceful act; it is a free gift and thus is virtuous, which makes it an energy of God.

When Susan and I operated Brother Juniper's Café, we set up a small prayer corner in the office section of our tiny kitchen. Before our employees (mostly high school students and developmentally disabled adults) came in each day we held a short prayer ritual in which we asked to be used as channels of grace in the lives of those who entered. We established certain patterns to help support us in this striving, playing uplifting music (usually classical or Celtic folk music), creating a small play area for children, carefully choosing the wall art and the like. Despite these important support structures we had many moments of crisis and disagreement surrounding management issues, cooking choices, short-temperedness, and other manifestations of fatigue and stress. We often felt like play actors, putting on happy, cheerful, courteous faces for customers when inside we were grappling with upset and anger. There were times when we were actually afraid to pray to be used by God because it seemed as if were setting ourselves up to realize our many inadequacies. We often wondered if we were failures as both restaurateurs and also as Christians. Despite the many difficult days and challenges to our personal sense of virtue and civility, we forged ahead knowing that our obligation to our customers was to model the courtesies that we espoused. Not being great actors we knew that our customers, many of them regulars, could tell when we were floundering, but they seemed to know we were making the effort. As a result, when we closed the café after Susan suffered a serious back injury and we knew we couldn't keep it going and also build our bakery business, some of the towns-people of Forestville actually presented us with a petition beseech-ing us to keep it open. Some of the locals offered to work as vol-unteers, especially those whose kids had worked for us. We received testimonials and even cash offers to keep it open.

This outpouring of affection and appreciation proved to us that grace can flow even through flawed vessels, which is the effi-cacy of synergy. The empowerment of the interior priesthood is derived only partially from our own efforts to practice virtue—the rest is the gift that exceeds us, it is the virtue that flows to-wards us as energy from God. We practice virtue not because we possess it, but so that we may receive it.

Thousands of books on the subject of empowerment have been written. A close look at them reveals a profoundly spiritual insight: The best of them are simply an elaboration and amplification of the Golden Rule—*do unto others as you would have them do unto you.* In other words, they teach the practice of virtues. I am continually amazed at how simple these deep mystery teachings and principles are: extensions of virtue.

From the perspective of sacred psychology, looking at prin-ciples of empowerment in the context of *theosis* and *religio,* we can see how clearly virtue relates to God-realization. The first thing is how significantly the word "others" appears. The operative spiri-tual principle, whether espoused by Mother Teresa, Father Paul, or throughout history by many saints and mystics, is that the fastest way to know God is to recognize and serve the God in others. By putting their needs and concerns before our own we immediately exercise the virtue of humility and *caritas* (love through selfless ser-vice, charity).

One day we had a first-time customer come into Brother Juniper's Café, and he had an attitude about him, very confrontational and edgy. He asked Susan a number of pointed questions concerning our order's views on sexuality and homosexuality in particular. She asked him back what he was getting at and he said, "What I really want to know is whether you serve customers who have AIDS?"

Her response was one of the most perfect comebacks I've ever heard, especially knowing how difficult this customer was acting. She said, "Look, when people come to the counter to order I ask them if they want hot, medium, or mild barbecue sauce, not if they have AIDS." It totally defused the situation and he even chuckled, a bit impressed, I think, with her quick-wittedness. It turned out that he was very active in taking meals to AIDS victims and had had some unpleasant experiences when bringing them into restaurants to eat. As a result of this encounter we became very involved in supporting our local AIDS support network and in developing relationships with a number of AIDS sufferers who became regulars. We were, sadly but I think inspirationally, the providers of final meals for some of our customers in their end stage, receiving thank you cards and messages for treating them with dignity and with food that they perceived as nourishing on many levels.

In our human-ness we may not always have totally pure motives when serving another, especially if we expect any kind of reward or payoff, but the very action initiates a whole series of events and draws back to the giver a reflection of what was given. In eastern religions it is called karma. Others call it the law of cause and effect. Like draws unto like. That which we give is in some manner, shape, or form given back in return. Susan, with her Catholic school background, puts it succinctly: What goes around comes around.

If, beyond the immediate material goals of personal success, our intent is meaningfulness, connectedness, and oneness with God, then actions of humility, civility, and service can heal our souls of the selfishness and pride that interfere with its attainment. Eventually, after frequent practice, which also means after many humility-inducing moments, even the motives begin to clear up. Practicing the virtues is a type of ongoing spiritual practice, not unlike the punch-down phase of bread making, and it is the logical extension of the formal prayers we say when we worship God and ask to be made channels of grace.

When we punch down bread dough, humbling it as a creation dependent upon the baker's beneficence and skill, it springs back, strengthened in flavor and character, building upon the fermentation already present. Letting some air out of the dough is a necessary passage if the dough is to become truly great bread.

Acquiring virtue develops in us the resiliency to continually spring back no matter how many times we are punched down by life's vicissitudes, developing our own flavor and character but also, and more importantly, laying the foundation for an empowerment of the soul. This empowerment is the activation of our interior priesthood, allowing the energies of God to enter the world through us in infinite, profound, and humble ways.

There can be no growth, no evoking of the fullness of our own (or our bread's) potential, without enduring punch downs. They lead to humility. But humility is a powerful creative force; it is a manifestation of one of the energies of God, and what could be more empowering than that?

5

Going Through
the Narrow Gate

*We should know that books can be understood, and ought to be
explained, in four principal senses. One is called literal, . . . the second
is called allegorical, . . . the third sense is called moral, . . . the fourth
sense is called anagogical (mystical). . . . And in such demonstration, the
literal sense should always come first, as that whose meaning includes all
the rest, and without which it would be impossible and irrational to
understand the others; and above all would it be impossible with the
allegorical. Because in everything which has an inside and an outside, it
is impossible to get at the inside, if we have not first got at the outside.*

Dante, Il Convito, II, 2–5

In the summer of 1981 I climbed Mount Shasta in northern
California for the first and only time. While not of the difficulty and danger of a Himalayan peak, or of a Mount McKinley
in Denali, Alaska, it was a significant achievement in my life. I was
beginning to see things in a multidimensional way, viewing events

as metaphors, with layers leading to deeper mystery. This is the journal entry I wrote after the climb:

The Mountain and the Magic

Mount Shasta is 14,162 feet high—less than half the height of Mount Everest yet still the 16th tallest mountain in the United States and second highest in California. It is considered either the northernmost mountain in the Sierra Range or the southernmost member of the Cascade Range. Either way, it is the last mountain in California before entering Oregon. Climbers refer to it as a "bear." I think of it as a place of magic.

Shasta has a reputation among those who profess to know of being a spiritual power spot. Few who have heard of Mount Shasta haven't also heard of the "green flash," St. Germaine and the ascended masters, who are supposed to dwell within or upon the mountain, the "golden escalator," which reputedly transports beings of the middle kingdom from the center of the mountain, or the reported landings of UFOs. Shasta is also known as a sacred mound for the local Native American tribes, where contact with their nature and ancestral spirits was favored. I missed all of these: no green flash, golden escalators, or UFOs graced our visit; we couldn't even find the local ritual sweat lodge. The ascended masters did not appear in person. However, I still believe that the mountain is magic.

Why? Because for me and for the six others who climbed with me to the summit, the world now looks somehow different. I don't believe the mountain did it to us, changed our perception, but climbing the mountain did. When we climbed Mount Shasta we stepped out of time and into archetype. One of the great symbols of spiritual quest, The Mountain, became a living reality and presented us with a specific adventure, uniquely suited to the needs of this seven-person fellowship. If we'd had eyes to see it and ears to hear it we would have known that we were conquering dragons and threshold dwellers, fed by elves, visited by angels, and guided by the hand of the unseen God. We didn't know it at the time but we were playing dungeons and dragons, not on a playing board but for real. We didn't realize it at the time because the only thing we did know was that climbing this mountain was hard, it hurt, we couldn't breathe, and we were scared. Our senses were tuned to survival, not fun and adventure. There was no way of recognizing the signs of magic, it was just happening around us. We entertained angels unaware and others threw their tent flaps wide open for us, but we didn't know.

Our fellowship formed out of friendship and a mutual desire to climb this mountain. We encouraged each other during the weeks preceding the climb to get into shape. We jogged, climbed local San Francisco hills, broke-in our Pivetta hiking boots, and looked over topological maps together. We also realized that there was nothing that could really prepare us adequately for the altitude and pain.

We met someone at the base camp who had just come down from a successful summit assault, and he warned us that it would hurt. Making it to the top was strictly a matter of mind and will, of deciding to put one foot in front of the other and refusing to quit. He said it was like running a marathon. He was right.

Our group arrived at the mountain on Thursday night so that we would have two nights of acclimatization before our Saturday assault. In reading the ledger of other climbers' accounts we discovered it is not unusual to spend a week acclimatizing. We had city, sea-level blood flowing through us when the climb began, but I felt we had mountain blood when we returned. Altitude sickness usually manifests as headache, nausea, cramps, and mental fatigue. We got it, but not as bad as some.

Only two of our party had ever climbed a glacier peak before, Ron and Elisabeth. Ron, being the most experienced, was chosen as climbing leader and would have final say in any situation.

As the time for the actual climb approached our individual concerns began to surface. What would happen if one or two didn't want to go on? Would we quit if our crampons (ice-walking cleats attached to our boots) should break; should we go on anyway? How will I feel if I'm the only one who doesn't want to go on? What if I fail? What if I die?

A bad omen, I fear, occurs: I burned our supper, a homemade campfire pot roast consisting of beef, turkey, potatoes, carrots, and onions. I didn't seal the foil properly and the meat burned instead of stewed. This is just the kind of thing that could ruin morale and send us to bed hungry and angry. Fortunately, Philip made a few loaves of excellent French bread (Julia Child's recipe) and we still had cheese and "gorp" (a wonderful combination of M&Ms, raisins, seeds, and nuts designed to give quick energy bursts and replenish carbohydrates). We went to bed content; I am forgiven. The magic is beginning.

Why is it, I wonder at our 3:00 A.M. prayer service, that God seems so close here every time my attention goes to Him? Is it the thin mountain air, the elevation? Afterwards, there is something stirring in me as I sit with my hot oatmeal and wheat berries thinking about this worship experience, this subtle knowledge that we are not alone. I'd been thinking about this ever since we got to base camp the day before and wondered if the others were as well. We had been avoiding too much spiritual talk, concentrating on the nuts and bolts of the climb, allowing our simple devotional practices to maintain the ecclesiastical balance, realizing that in nature God's beauty and power is reflected more clearly than in the confusion of city life. Yet, I wondered if this were the only reason God felt so close as I tried to remember other camp-outs in the wilderness. Was it always like this? I couldn't recall.

James, with the wit and humor born of encroaching anxiety, reminded us that he was seriously scared and we shouldn't worry if he panicked. "I came, I saw, I sniveled," he said, striking the pose of a scared Caesar. There had already been, with more to come, such quips, each of us sublimating the tension of our personal fears into humorous comments. However, we also knew the axiom, "Much truth is said in jest," and this betrayed us to each other. Since we were all in the same boat we didn't care. In a fellowship there are understandings that need not be spoken, there is empathy and, as in the burnt supper, forgiveness.

Philip was much stronger than the rest of us. The mountain could not contain his energy as he forged ahead of us during the first phase, working our way up rock and talus to Lake Helen at 10,400 feet. His body, strong and agile, glided up the rock while mine seemed to be working against me as if a constant reminder to my brain that gravity would not be mocked. We spread out, each discovering his or her own pace. Somehow I lost the path as I observed to my left other climbers going up a different route, seemingly easier. What's more, I lost sight of Philip. The others were behind me and I was leading them up a false path. Early panic set in. "Ron, I think I blew it."

His response was calm and secure. "It's okay, all these paths lead to the same place." Another moment of magic missed.

We finally came together at Lake Helen (not really a lake anymore, just a flat spot that served as a universal rendezvous point). The pattern of the climb was established: Philip was walking up a piece of cake; Ron, the best climber, staying back, safely escorting James and Rebekah, who were on their first climb; Michael, Elisabeth, and I were somewhere in the middle.

We were walking up ice now, our crampons giving traction and our ice axes giving support. I was ahead of everyone except Phil and, when I turned around, noticed everyone else stopped around James, about 200 feet downhill. His crampon broke, a screw had come out. Would we go on, send him back, return as one, what? Wait a minute, what's this! A stranger, a girl, is catching up to me. Her face is smeared with sun block glacier cream, making her look like Al Jolson in "The Jazz Singer." She is climbing without gloves, without an ice ax, and without crampons. "Hi! Isn't this incredible?" she hums, and breezes by as I wait for word from below.

Michael and Ron rig up something to make James's crampon work. We all continue, passing the white-faced minstrel as she scrambles, her hands in the snow, a small tent pole serving as an ax. "You have got to be kidding," I mumble to no one in particular.

It is now noon and we have all arrived at the foot of the Red Banks. All, that is, except Rebekah, who, with a ghastly pained and contorted look on her face, is taking the final steps to our rendezvous. A few of us look at each other, asking with eye contact the unspoken question. Elisabeth answers: "She wouldn't turn back now for anything. She's a very strong-willed person."

Phil adds, "She's German."

I wonder at the implication of this, my mind flashing wildly at all my associations having to do with Germans. The altitude is making us all a little bit crazy here at 12,000 feet. Somehow, Rebekah's making it to the Red Banks causes me to suddenly admire Germany, knowing that it is indeed her birthplace.

"Hi! Isn't this fantastic!" I hear the voice of "Al Jolson" who is here too! She made it this far though I can't, for the life of me, figure out how.

"Planning to spend the rest of the day here?" I snottily ask.

"Are you kidding? I've come this far, I'm going to the top!" I decide she must be German too. "By the way," she continues, "are you from the Bay Area?" Assured that we are she asks, "Could I catch a ride home with you? My friend left last night but I just had to make the climb."

I hear a growl from somewhere nearby, I think it was Elisabeth. Our nonverbal exchange is clear but this is no time to work out a difference of opinion, especially since Al Jolson was always a favorite singer of mine. Ron and I give her the standard "Let's see how it goes" routine. Who is this weird person, anyway? A white-faced, summertime halter-topped, crampon-less flower child climbing Mount Shasta and somehow assuming herself into our party, our fellowship, without an invitation, without even an ice ax. Oh God! I offer her some gorp and logan bread.

Philip wants to get on to the next leg, up the narrow chute through the Red Banks—1000 feet straight up. I hate him and love him at the same time. He, Michael, Elisabeth, and I take off first, giving Rebekah, James, and Ron a few minutes more to rest. James entertains us with "Why me, Lord?" routines, as he tells us about his crampon miseries. We laugh, we cry, we push on. We expect to see him make it to the top of the chute even though I know for a fact that he is not German.

This is the hardest part for me; every step requires two breaths. I throw my ax in front and pull myself up. It hurts, I'm dizzy. I flash on our early worship service and suddenly there's a wind inside me, a will, and the voice of yesterday's climber, "Just gotta' decide to put one foot in front of the other." Who was he and how did his voice get wrapped up in my worship experience? More magic, but no strength left to marvel at it.

One hundred feet from the crest I get faint. Quickly, proud of my fast thinking, I pull out my lone Jack LaLanne Trail Mix Bar and take a bite with each step. What a great commercial this would have made. Blood sugar restored, I pull myself over the crest.

Philip is already changed into other clothes and resting. The others gradually arrive, including Deborah, the white-faced minstrel. "Hi! Isn't this a kick?" She then goes off to talk with some other climbers resting on this butte, probably asking them if they're from the Bay Area.

James stumbles over the crest, too tired to wisecrack. Rebekah follows, too stubborn to give up. My heart is experiencing something; my head does not recognize magic, it's too busy finding ways to soothe my aching body.

Philip, our champion, has lost his magnificent color. I hear him mutter, "My mood has completely changed." After nine hours he's finally hit the wall, and about time, I think. I'm glad he now knows what the rest of have been experiencing for hours. Nevertheless, he and Elisabeth and I start out on the final assault, the last 1200 feet. Philip falls behind for the first time. I hear him say, "This mountain sure takes the ego out of you." He's right.

We've been climbing almost ten hours now; my body has never been this worn out, my head is ringing, worship is a distant dream . . . what! I'm thinking about it. The wind blows again within me and, again, I don't feel alone. Time doesn't exist; the past ten hours accordion into one splitting headache, a simple symbol of an arduous effort, but I know now that we are all going to make the summit!

I pass a frozen robin perched on a snow bank, a dead sentinel with beak pointing to the top. Then I see a honeybee, always a sign of paradoxical wonder to me, encased in snow crystals, facing the summit as if to say, "Oh death, where is thy sting?" We're walking upon a once cavernous volcano crater, looking down into another crater belonging to Shastina, the smaller companion-mountain of Shasta. Phil is catching up; he's caught his second wind too and wants to be our champion again. We approach the final scree pile, a hill that reeks of sulfur. I remember hearing that somewhere around here John Muir once weathered a blizzard by cozying into a smelly sulfur spring in one of the volcanic cracks.

Looking down, I see the other climbers spread out like the proverbial knights on white satin. I see Michael, the silent steady one, catching up with Elisabeth and, behind them, James and Ron, then Rebekah. Parallel to them, forging her own path, comes a singular white-faced figure. This moment, I recognize now, is another freeze-frame of magic.

Phil scrambles over the top and disappears. By the time I join him on the razor peak he is perched atop the highest rock talking with a fellow conqueror from another group. There are a few men already on the top. They were part of a Christian group who'd been on their own vision quest.

Next over the top I hear the voice of Deborah: "Hi! Isn't this incredible?" It is.

Soon we are all together on the summit. The incredulity of the moment doesn't fully register. Only now, in retrospect, am I indelibly impressed. This is a moment frozen out of time and space, truly a peak experience, fusing the bonds of our fellowship into what must surely be a kind of forever-ness.

Glissading down the mountain (i.e., sliding on our butts using the ice ax as a rudder and a brake) was pure reward. Before we began James confided that going down scared him as much as going up. Halfway down the chute leading back to the Red Banks a large rock jutted into the glissade track. I just missed hitting it and decided to wait there for the others to warn them. Deborah came barreling down, using her little tent pole to steer.

She stopped in time and I helped her past the rock. She continued to the end of the chute where Phil was waiting. I saw him
point the way, saw her sit down in the grooved snow, and slide
away, disappearing into a speck, then lost amidst the stones. It
was the last we would see of her this day.

Then Ron, Michael, James, Elisabeth, and Rebekah all came
down together, one behind the other. I warned them of the
rock. Ron, correctly cautious, felt that the ice was too slick to
control our speed so he asked everyone to walk down along the
side of the groove. Suddenly, Rebekah slipped and fell into the
chute. In one movement, and it seems like slow motion to me
now as I recall it, Ron and James grabbed her, Ron's pack falling
off and sliding down the groove to where I stood, able to catch
it. I wondered if Rebekah would have been so easy to stop had it
been her. There was now a new feeling in the air. Rebekah,
though no longer in any real danger, couldn't see that she was
safe and so she was tensing up, intensely concentrating. James
held her from above and Ron from below. Michael came over
and the three of them were able to hoist her back onto the snow.
Once past the rock, she and Ron slid down together, piggyback
style, till clear of the chute. Another bond forged.

I remember watching James throw himself towards Rebekah
to catch her during the fall, and how all three men were concentrating on rescuing her from her situation. The fear that James
expressed before the glissade was gone from him, consumed in
the fire of his selfless act. This was a precious moment. The rest
of the journey down for James was done fearlessly.

It took three hours to descend Shasta after spending eleven
hours going up.

Michael fell asleep as soon as we hit camp. The rest of us ate
canned beef stew; I didn't burn it this time but my body was

completely burned out. My mind, however, was wide awake. Phil and I stayed up later than the others, sitting around the fire, reliving the climb. We talked about a group of men and women we had met going up, at Lake Helen. They carried long poles with decorative feathers on them. I thought they must be Indians. The leader was 79 years old and he was going up for the 25th time, taking his sons, daughters, and a niece with him. It is hard to imagine how a man of 79 could handle what lay ahead. It was also humbling. I think sitting around the fire with Phil was the beginning of the realization of magic. I cried for the first time, just a little tear here and there, and I went to sleep feeling very close to everyone.

In the morning I went to get water to wash the pots. At the spring I heard a familiar voice. "Hi! Isn't this an incredible morning!" It was Deborah without glacier cream; I could finally see her face. She was beautiful. "Guess what! I got a ride home. I met a man at Lake Helen, 79 years old. He's going to take me home after he finishes his climb today. Last night he let me sleep in his teepee between him and his daughter. I didn't have a sleeping bag or anything. Isn't that a kick!"

I brought her back to the camp, sorry that someone else, even this crazy 79-year-old Indian, should be taking her home instead of us. Everyone greeted her like long lost friends and we loaded her up with fruit and gorp and eggs. She gave me a hug before returning up the hill to Lake Helen to wait for the old man to return. I asked her, "Deborah, what kind of Indian is he?"

She said, "Oh, he's no Indian, he just likes to make feather talismans and sell them." And then she was gone.

It wasn't until we arrived home, after hamburgers and milk shakes along the way, stopping to take pictures against the backdrop of Mount Shasta and the nearby hills called Castle Crags, that I began to believe in the magic. When our friends at home asked about the trip it was hard to describe it without feeling that somehow we had participated in something terribly important, extraordinary even, but not because of the climbing accomplishment. When Ron, Michael, James, and I had some time alone to talk it was hard to do so without tears. Ron was different than I'd ever seen him. I asked him if all mountain climbing trips produced this feeling and he said he'd never felt anything like this before.

This is what I felt and I write it down, a few weeks after the climb, so that I will never forget:

I felt loved and because I felt loved I also felt able to love. Shasta did not love us but on Shasta love touched us. I believe we realized, just as Dorothy discovered on the road to Oz, that you don't have to leave home to find the rainbow. Occasionally, though, when the wind blows right, the rainbow finds you and gives you a glimpse of the world of possibilities, the reality of the quest, the unquestioning reality of God's love as raw power—raw as a mountain and just as impersonal. Impersonal, that is, until it flows into you through the Rons, Elisabeths, James, Phils, Rebekahs, and Michaels who share the journey with you—who personalize it. And through the white-faced Deborahs, who mysteriously appear—and disappear—so that we might never forget "lest we entertain angels in disguise." I will always believe that the mountain is magic.

(From My Journal: August, 1981)

The multitextured reality of life, the layer upon layer of meaning in each moment, is not always so vivid as it was on that climb, even though every moment in life is ripe with such opportunity.

There are times, and we have all had them, when everything seems suddenly clear, even if for just a fleeting moment, and when that happens it invokes a kind of accountability. As I climbed from the broad base to the narrow peak of Shasta I understood that my own path was narrowing. Going deep was no longer one of many options but was now a requirement if I were to grow and fulfill the yearning awakened years before on Highway 80. If my life was to be played out on many levels, then I needed to become conscious of my choices on as many of those levels as possible because I now understood that as we intensify the depth of our perception we pass certain points of no return.

I began paying closer attention to how my outside adventures reflected my inner theostic quest, using them as signposts of my journey toward an interior priesthood and the realization of myself in the image and likeness of God. Bread, which by now had become my livelihood, also became my guiding metaphor and a tool to navigate me through the four levels that Dante described. Unlike climbing a mountain, a one-time event in my life, it gave me an ongoing daily *outside*, a literal situation through which to get at the figurative *inside* of my journey.

Weighing or *scaling*, for instance, is when dough is divided into the individual pieces that will eventually become the loaves. It represents a narrowing of the process, the movement from bulk to individual, from the broad to the deep, in the same way that the path we are on begins to narrow as we see more deeply into its implications.

San Giuseppe Bread

It is no coincidence that nearly every religious holiday has a bread associated with it. From the unleavened matzoh of

Passover to the elaborate fruited breads like stollen and *panet-tone* of Christmas, bread signifies God's presence in the world, the universal symbol of life. Many of the Christian festivals, even the lesser-known ones celebrated in honor of patron and local saints, have special breads. For example, San Giuseppe bread is a wonderful Italian loaf made in honor of Joseph, the father of Jesus. The dough is not complex, a slightly en-riched soft bread, but the way it is shaped is what makes it unique. The strands represent the beard of St. Joseph, and the loaf does, indeed, look like a man's beard.

Breads like this help to tell a story and provide a means of transmission of knowledge from generation to generation, teaching a worldview to children through the joys of food, music, and dance, which bypass the usual intellectual processes and, instead, create flavor and sense memories that nourish and sustain us far beyond the original event. Bread, like other symbols, thus becomes a peg of our unfolding souls on which experiences can be hung.

Mise en Place

Makes 1 large loaf or 2 small loaves

3 ¹/₂ *cups bread or all-purpose flour* (unbleached if possible)

1 ¹/₂ *teaspoons salt* (2 ¹/₂ teaspoons if using kosher salt)

1 *tablespoon instant yeast* (or 1 ¹/₄ tablespoons active dry yeast dissolved in ¹/₄ cup of warm milk)

1 *cup whole or low-fat milk* (heated to lukewarm, plus additional if needed)

4 *tablespoons butter* (melted)

1 *egg, beaten* (for wash)

Poppy seeds (for garnishing the top)

Mixing and Primary Fermentation

Mix all the ingredients together (except for the poppy seeds) in a large bowl until they form a coarse ball of dough. Add more milk if the dough seems stiff. If it is too sticky, that can be adjusted during the kneading. Turn the dough ball out onto a lightly floured counter or work surface and begin kneading the dough. Add flour if necessary, or a few dribbles of milk if it still feels too stiff. Knead the dough for about ten minutes. It should form a soft, pliable dough, tacky but not sticky. It should be easy to stretch and pull. If not, add more milk. The dough will be slightly warm and seem quite springy.

Place the dough in a lightly greased bowl, cover with a moist towel or with plastic wrap, and allow to ferment for about one hour, or till doubled in size.

Punching Down, Weighing, Rounding, Resting, and Shaping

For a single loaf, divide the dough into the following pieces: 1 piece weighing 10 ounces, 2 pieces weighing 5 ounces each, 2 pieces weighing 2 $^1/_2$ ounces each. If making 2 loaves, make each of these pieces half the size. Roll out each piece of dough into a strand. The largest strand should be about 8 inches long. The next largest should be about 6 inches long (they will be thinner), and the smallest should be about 4 inches long. Lay the largest strand in the middle of a sheet pan that has been covered with baking parchment. Next, lay the middle-sized strands along each side of the big piece, even across the top and touching down the sides. (They will be shorter than the center piece at the bottom.) Do the same with the smallest strands, again placing them even across the top and ending them shorter at the sides. Brush the top of the dough with well-beaten egg and sprinkle with poppy seeds. Place the pan inside a plastic trash bag and allow to proof at room temperature for about 45 minutes, or until nearly doubled in size.

Baking, Cooling, and Eating or Storing

Preheat the oven to 350 degrees (300 degrees if convection). Place the sheet pan in the oven and bake for approximately 30 minutes, or until the loaf is golden brown and firm and springy to the touch (the internal temperature of the center strand should be approximately 185 degrees if you have a thermometer). Cool on a rack for at least 20 minutes before serving. The bread may be either sliced or pulled apart by strands. If storing, wrap it completely in plastic wrap and keep in a cool, dark place or freeze.

Brother Juniper's Café was kind of like the bulk dough of the many Brother Juniper's projects, only one of which was bread. When the bakery spun off from the café, it was because the bread production we did for our own use had outgrown our facility. The café was so small that all we had room for was a refrigerator for the fresh products. During the first year we made small batches of bread dough the evening before we needed it, putting the shaped, unbaked loaves into a pick-up truck when we went home each evening, transporting it back to the retreat center where it could be chilled in the walk-in refrigerator. The following morning we drove the dough back to the café where it was baked and served.

The café was located in an arcade of small shops, one of which was a flower store. The owner of the store took pity on us after watching the daily dough migration and suggested we use part of her walk-in refrigerator, which was underutilized as a flower chiller. This was a great solution, allowing us to simply walk the pans of shaped dough across the hall, saving time and energy. This arrangement worked well for us for about a year, but our production was gradually increasing, using up more and more of the flower shop's refrigerator space. Other restaurants were asking us to make struan and other breads for them, and we could hardly refuse, needing as much cash flow as possible to keep our small operation afloat.

We began sensing that we were running out of space and time as both our business and the flower shop's business continued to grow. The defining moment occurred when the owner of the flower shop came in to tell us that she had been wondering why her roses were drooping sooner than they ought to and so had called a flower merchant who asked her what else was in the walk-in with the roses. When she told him bread dough he hit the roof. "Don't you know that yeast kills roses!" he shouted at her. So that was the end of a pretty good thing, but it forced us to consider our options, the best one being the renting of a space around the corner that had been a small bakery about to go out of business. We not only bought all the equipment that was there but also managed to keep the baker and add her to our staff, where she was a mainstay for many years.

Within another year Brother Juniper's Bakery had so outgrown the café that when we closed the café we were producing nearly a thousand loaves a day, selling them throughout northern California. Two years later we were forced to move again into an even larger facility in Santa Rosa, and I wrote my first book, *Brother Juniper's Bread Book: Slow Rise as Method and Metaphor*, riding the bread metaphor ever deeper into my destiny. When Susan and I sold the bakery in 1993, we were producing nearly two thousand loaves a day and had become local culinary celebrities. Struan had been the primary wagon that we rode, opening up teaching and writing opportunities that continue to unfold. The scaling of our initial project called Brother Juniper's Café into a singular expression focused on breads, was the turning point for my career as a baker, writer, and a Christian lay brother. The convergence of ingredients turned into an interesting loaf.

Having discovered a very personal expression and metaphor to enliven my sense of purpose and meaningfulness, what I then sought was a deepening of my religious framework to support it. The very idea of a physical, mental, and spiritual realization of myself in the image and likeness of God is both a profound and threatening concept. Jesus and most of his apostles were killed for suggesting that such a possibility existed, as were many other spiritual pioneers. It is a journey fraught with the possibility of self-deception and egomania, a tightrope walk. Without proper guidance and direction a soul could get quite lost in search of *theosis*.

As the gates narrowed, I had traversed from the wonderfully idiosyncratic spirituality of Father Paul's order to the more traditional path of Eastern Orthodoxy. My spiritual direction now was to be drawn from the wisdom of the historical church. In Orthodoxy the journey of the soul is described as a path of ascetic struggle, a process of purification that enables one to handle the challenges that inevitably come as the quest unfolds. Nikitas Stithatos (in "On the Practice of the Virtues," no. 13, *The Philokalia*, vol. 4) expressed it this way 1500 years ago: To master the mundane will of the fallen self you have to fulfill three conditions. First, you have to overcome avarice by embracing the law of righteousness, which consists in merciful compassion for one's fellow beings; second, you have to conquer self-indulgence through prudent self-restraint, that is to say, through all-inclusive self-control; and third, you have to prevail over your love of praise through sagacity and sound understanding, in other words through exact discrimination in things human and divine, trampling such love underfoot as something cloddish and worthless. All this you have to do until the mundane will is converted into the law of the spirit of life and liberated from domination by the law of the outer fallen self. Then you can say, 'I thank God that the law of the spirit of life has freed me from the law and dominion of death.'

A process of purification, the battle for virtue, is a lifelong struggle. Since we never know the time and place that our epiphanies will come we rarely feel ready or worthy when they do. The insight I gleaned from my search for a sacred psychology, and from the sacred psychologists and spiritual elders who serve as its guides, is that everyone is born with the yearning, passion, and potential to connect with God. Throughout life unforeseen factors often interfere with the intensity of this desire and many of us lose the spiritual yearning for religio, regaining it only briefly from time to time. Sometimes we make choices that distance us so much from our spiritual intuition that we fall into a path called, among other names, evil, and become lost souls.

The spiritually wise know that each soul, no matter how lost, has the potential to be awakened and redeemed. The most helpful offering to a lost soul, or even to ourselves when we feel lost, is an encounter with virtue, a taste of unconditional love. Virtue is far more convincing than any words of advice—it is an expression of the energy of God; it touches us at the soul level, it is the vessel of that unconditional love.

When I was just beginning to practice religion I discovered a small yet profound book called *The Practice of the Presence of God*. It tells the story of Brother Lawrence, a simple Carmelite lay-brother of seventeenth-century Paris, a cook (of course), who influenced others through a zen-like approach to Christian spiritual practice. His practice was based on living in the moment, secure

87

that God is always present, that there is meaning in each experience, and that God witnesses and guides us at all times. Brother Lawrence's principles of living are encapsulated in the following quote: "The time of business does not with me differ from the time of prayer, and in the noise and clatter of my kitchen, while several persons are at the same time calling for different things. I possess God in as great tranquility as if I were upon my knees at the blessed sacrament. . . . Many do not advance in the Christian progress because they stick in penances and particular exercises, while they neglect the love of God, which is the *end*."

Though I have been a brother and a pilgrim for over twenty-five years, I believe my most spiritual year was the first. As a novice I was under only one vow: obedience. The novitiate period was clearly about purification and the striving for virtue. The novices wash dishes, they have little or no say in the running of things, they take orders from anyone with seniority, and they take careful pains to address everyone respectfully. They simply try harder. I observed in both myself and in others how the intensity of this striving changed as more freedom and powers were given to us while we progressed through the various training stages and temporary vows, culminating in the taking of our final vows of service, purity, poverty, and humility, as well as the original vow of obedience. These five vows were meant to signify even greater striving, but I think they actually delineated a much more formal internal structure, a framework for our striving in recognition that, over time and with freedom, the intensity of striving tends to diminish.

One of the great challenges for anyone on the religious path is maintaining focus, and the structure of one's denomination is supposed to support this, guiding us through the ever narrowing gates towards our heart's goal. Some people manage to grow in their ascetic labors while many others, for various reasons, begin to slacken off until they either leave or find a comfort level that matches their degree of internal fire (or lack of). One of the reasons that villages were once built with monasteries at their center is because of the symbolism of radiating layers of theostic intensity. While union with God is not limited or reserved for monks, they are the ones who symbolize a life totally dedicated to its pursuit, the soul alone with God.

Here is the challenge we now face: We already know what we need to know; knowledge is not the problem, wisdom is. Bearing spiritual knowledge wisely is a result of proper formation, discipline, and purification of the soul, and it adheres to a proscribed method and practice. If it is spiritual warfare, metaphorical or not, who or what is it we are fighting? It is a fight against anything that prevents us from our goal, which is the experience of who we are in relation to our Source, to mystical union with God, *theosis*, deification, or, in existential terms, to a sense of meaning and purpose for our existence. If our goal is truth of self, then the enemy is self-deception.

Prelest is the Slavonic term for such delusion. It is attributed to overly trusting in ourselves instead of God. Guarding against *prelest* is a theme that repeats in every traditional spiritual training manual. The path of spiritual warfare is a striving for virtue, a means of purification in which one is strengthened to bear the weight of deeper levels of self-knowledge. The acquisition of virtue as we go through the narrow gates of our chosen paths is a vital aspect of sacred psychology because it addresses directly the formation of the soul, the seat of the moral and mystical dimension of our understanding. Without a healthy soul any notion of spiritual attainment is extremely dangerous.

Going through the narrow gate is like passing through the looking glass, falling into the hole that leads to another world. It is a passage into vertical realities, quite different from the horizontal-

89

ness of daily existence. It is when we realize we are priestly heroes in our own mythopoetic sagas, souls enwrapped by a body, on a journey in which every choice is significant, every encounter linked to a larger tableau. Worlds exist within worlds and, to our astonishment, everything matters and leads to something else that matters even more. It is the realm of true sacramental magic in our everyday lives, and we are each priestly magi in search of the elusive star.

6

Integrating the Inner
and Outer Person

In the fall of 1994, at the age of forty-four, while contemplating my own integration and growth cycles, I wrote an article for a local newspaper where I was a semiregular contributor to the Religion and Ethics page. It was partly inspired by my remembrances of working with teenagers in North Carolina and also by similar patterns I was observing in teenagers of the '90s, the so-called street punks. It brought the most response of any piece I had written and included the following:

> . . . there is a strong spiritual reason that I, and perhaps
> many of my generation, are experiencing a yearning to re-
> connect with part of our past, our youth. Though it seems
> to adults that so many young people are lost, naive, or just
> confused, something very positive and necessary is taking
> place in the formation of their souls, and this, I am certain,
> is what is so compelling about this period. My theory is
> this: Somewhere between the ages of 18–24, plus or minus
> a few years on either side, the need to become an indepen-

dent, whole person emerges. To young adults, adult society seems flawed. During this period, perhaps for the first and clearest time, it is obvious that adults have compromised the purity of life's potential. Initiations like falling in love, discovering the beauty of nature, glimpsing a human, transcultural brotherhood, and the revelation of hypocrisy in all its forms make this the singlemost spiritually receptive period in a person's life. For many youth this experience is heightened by exposure to dramatic situations, significant mentors, new ideas through art and literature, and, for some, drugs. To many it seems as if scales were falling off their eyes, as if they were no longer seeing through a glass darkly.

92

The only problem is that a young adult's life experience is not sufficiently deep or broad enough. There is no context for understanding. These are days of confusion—but a glorious confusion in which the simple answer to everything is *love*. Why, young people ask, is this not abundantly clear to the rest of the world, especially the adult world?

And then follows the search for context, for meaning, for identity—whether it be religious, political, career, or sexual.

Years later, as fully formed adults, we realize that we have become what we reviled or judged so harshly. We have, each of us, made our own compromises, exercised our judgments on our neighbors and enemies, embarked upon a career path, or two, and raised children of our own, many of whom are now entering that critical initiatic phase just described. Little by little the clarity of our own hypersensitive youth has been replaced by activities and careers; our surviving connections with that time are remnants like music, and we begin to wonder why some songs that were so important back then no longer trigger the same emotions or catharses.

Our youthful confusion has been replaced with a slightly cynical certainty of how things are, steeped in a worldview of conclusions and rules. The earlier period seems like a dream; the earlier person seems like someone else.

By an act of grace we reach another time in life, during our mid-forties, give or take a few years on either side, when a longing stirs for a taste of that youthful vision, that confused clarity. We try to fight it because we are convinced it is too late to start over, we have become established, but the yearning persists. Slackers, Gen X'ers, punkers, hippies, beatniks, whatever the name the pattern's the same. We realize, if we are not revolted by the revolts of youth, that buried somewhere amidst the various costumes, uniforms, attitudes, and styles is a seed in search of sunlight, a self in search of hope—a hope for a better, more meaningful world.

It is amazing that the better world most young people cry out for is in perfect conformity with the vision of heaven as espoused by Jesus and other great religious leaders. Rebellion happens because to youth it is natural to be religious about love, while adults simply love to be religious. Religion fraught with compromise, politics, and hypocrisy seems phony to a youth who simply wants to love, unfettered by rules. It is clear, in hindsight, that there has to be a middle ground where the two can meet, which is what growing up is all about—the search for that place of balance.

As an emerging adult the yearning is to be free. As a middle adult the yearning, tempered by a few years of choices and compromises, is to be free again, but with the wisdom of hindsight. I am curious to see what the yearning will be during the next cycle, for the senior adult who has passed through it all and, perhaps, made his or her peace with the whole process.

❧ ⸺ ⸻ ❧

As I reached my middle years and found myself back in the world, now a lay brother rather than a renunciate brother, married and with a business, the nature of cycles became evident. While life has a chronologically linear quality it also has a cyclical one as our souls unfold. Years of training for one vocation were being channeled and reinterpreted into another and I was beginning to appreciate the appropriateness of it all. I reconciled myself to the very real fact that the previous twenty years had been my training period, like going to a university, and now I had to go out and do something with it. So I became a teacher of what I knew best, bread, and decided to approach my career as a ministry instead of ministry as a career.

This crossroads in my life is similar to the sixth stage of bread production, called *rounding*. Rounding is when the individually scaled pieces of dough are shaped into balls or torpedoes in anticipation of a final shaping still to come. The point of rounding is to gather the dough in, bringing it together so it can begin the process of its final outward growth. This gathering in for the purpose of expressing out is very similar to the spiritual initiation of integrating our inner and outer selves. This integration is very much a function of building upon our growth as we complete one cycle in prelude to awaiting another round.

The process of integrating spiritual values into everyday life is, of course, another opportunity to sacramentalize everyday life. At Brother Juniper's we had an ideal venue in which to practice the priestly arts. Festival times were especially ripe for Susan. She would decorate the café with specially collected seasonal props and symbols. She arranged for some of the woodsmen in our community to cut boughs from our forest and brought in some of the more artistic Sisters to paint the windows and create spectacular Christmas scenes. St. Patrick's Day was another of her favorite times, with themes of green and Irish food to match. Festivals, though, are easier to draw upon than normal days, so our challenge was to approach every day as a festival, though in nonobvious ways. The children's area was particularly inspired; a simple rocking chair, some appropriate story books, a few pillows, and just the right kind of pictures mounted close to the floor created a safe place for young children to hang out while their parents enjoyed their meals.

The tables were few; we could only seat eighteen to twenty-four people at a time, which forced our customers to get creative and sensitive to each other, often voluntarily sharing tables so others wouldn't have to wait. When the lines were long, Susan or one of our high school employees would go out with pitchers of ginger fizz, one of our homemade sodas, and refresh the waiting crowds. These were just simple courtesies, but they were anchored in our daily prayer to be channels of light and grace. They worked beautifully from the customer's standpoint, creating an environment in which communion-like meals were enjoyed, nurturing our guests on many levels.

This all sounds very idyllic but the toll it took upon us to maintain the level of atmosphere that had become our standard was enormous. We worked so hard that fatigue began to wear us down. One of our vendors, Stan, a salesman from a food supplier, told me during our first month of operation how he appraised a restaurant's stability. He said, "It feels great in here right now, everything's clean and crisp and all the lights work. When I walk into a restaurant the first thing I check are the lights, to see if any of the bulbs have blown out and not been changed. When you stop noticing blown light bulbs, it's a sign that your energy is running down. It's all about energy."

His insight made such an impression on me that every week, when I knew that Stan was scheduled to come in to take our order, I checked the lights to make sure they were all lit. Later, during our third year, when Susan had blown her back out from the daily pressure and I was running back and forth between the café and the new bakery around the corner, I ran into Stan on the street as he was leaving, having taken the order from one of our other managers. He said, "One of the bulbs is out on the wagon wheel fixture. Are you okay?" Shortly after that was when we decided it might be time to close the café to focus on the bakery. Stan was right, our energy had simply run out.

A few years later, having sold the entire company when our remaining energy reserves were running on fumes, I faced a situation in which I would need to have the sacramentalizing quality of the interior priesthood so integrated in my being that it would express in environments no longer completely under our control. No longer aflame with the youthful religious-about-love fire, I set about trying to love my religion without becoming self-righteous about it. I always admired people who lived their values rather than talking about them; I wanted to be that kind of person. The natural cycle of integration, the convergence of previous adventures into yet another new expression, was upon me. To understand myself more thoroughly and to function discreetly, I was impelled to examine my values closely so I could express them appropriately in my new setting. I was no longer Doug, no longer Peter, nor even Brother Peter, but was now called Chef Peter. I had been cut from the bulk dough and was establishing an identity apart from the brotherhood. My outer life was now more in the world, which meant that my inner life was more important than ever. I needed a spiritual prayer practice to provide interior support and structure.

I think of formal, recitative prayers like grains of yeast in an otherwise full loaf of activities and thoughts. This leaven influences our lives, but we also contradict ourselves and nullify our prayers throughout the day with other thoughts, prayers, and actions. We think self-canceling thoughts and receive the commensurate results. St. Paul, in Thessalonians 5:17, says, "Pray without ceasing," but since I believe that every thought is a prayer, which means I already am praying without ceasing, Saint Paul's words take on another implication. They serve as a warning to pray and think wisely. Interior dialogue is, like it or not, a form of interior prayer. In my personal journey, and the journey of the Holy Order of MANS becoming Christ the Saviour Brotherhood, we discovered that there are powerful, traditional methodologies for structured interior prayer. One method is The Prayer of the Heart.

This ancient prayer was first brought to the attention of western readers in the book *The Way of the Pilgrim*, a Russian novel by an anonymous author. In that book a young Russian man, struggling with a sense of emptiness, embarks on a lifelong quest for meaning, encountering various degrees of helpfulness along the way. At one point he is taught The Prayer of the Heart, also called The Jesus Prayer, by an elder. The simple repetitive prayer, which is the most well-known element of the Hesychast tradition of orthodoxy, dating back to the twelfth century, goes: "Lord Jesus Christ, Son of God, have mercy on me, a sinner." It is an outgrowth of Saint Paul's admonition to "pray without ceasing," and is used in much the same way as a meditation mantra. The goal is to keep the prayer going at all times until it becomes so integrated into one's being that it changes from a primarily mental prayer into what is called a heart prayer. When achieved, this is known as bringing the mind into the heart. Its effectiveness, according to tradition, is based on the repeating of the name of Jesus, because:

"Whatsoever ye ask the Father in my name, He will give it to you" (John 16:23, 24).

The Jesus Prayer is a conscious application of synergy, an attempt on our part to draw to us the grace of God through a never-ending litany of yearning. Like other repetitive prayer practices, such as the Catholic rosary, the Buddhist Nam Yho Renge Kyo, the yogic and Sikh Sat Nam, the dozens of Transcendental Meditation (TM) mantras, and even the Hare Krishna chant, repeating the prayer is a petition from our soul for an experience of union with God. This creates a vacuum that gradually and in unforeseen and unpredictable ways draws experiences and opportunities to fulfill the intent of the prayer. This, of course, is a rather simple explanation of a more theologically complex and elaborate process. The Jesus Prayer is an example of a traditional spiritual method that initiates the full religious possibility, beginning in yearning and ending in mystical union with God.

For centuries, until the publication of *The Way of the Pilgrim*, few outside of serious Eastern Orthodox initiates or monks knew of The Jesus Prayer. It was considered too powerful and precious, even dangerous, to bestow on those who were not properly prepared or deemed worthy. It is not the words, for surely these are not the most crucial aspect of The Jesus Prayer, but the intent to walk the path, as in so many fairytales, that leads through dark, scary forests and deep, cold waters.

An old saying goes: Mysticism started in mist and ended in schism. My admonition to anyone who decides to do The Prayer of the Heart is to realize that motives are crucial. A pilgrim should ask him- or herself, "What is it I really hope to get by doing this practice? Am I prepared for the consequences? If I am not a Christian, am I prepared to become one, to accept a redemptive relationship with Jesus who, after all, is the focus of this prayer? Or, am I looking for a convincing phenomenological experience, like seeing auras or developing personal powers such as reading people's minds?" (If so, then this is not the prayer for you.) If the seeker is a confirmed Jew, Hindu, or Muslim, the person should seek out a practice within that tradition rather than doing The Jesus Prayer.

The critical assumption behind The Jesus Prayer is relationship with a personal Lord. The Judeo-Christian God is not simply a spiritual principle but an actual Being. An encounter with this Being is personal, not impersonal. Sacred psychology is premised upon this relationship, not simply upon a doctrine or philosophy. One question that brings it all into sharp focus is this: Would I be willing to go to the lions for my beliefs? Without a relationship that is personal and meaningful, I can guarantee that doctrine alone is not compelling enough to die for.

The Russian Orthodox church calls it a *podvig*, the personal struggle for a relationship with God that if embraced ultimately leads to holiness by stripping away the illusion of prideful individualism, replacing it with virtues such as humility, penitence, obedience, charitableness, and selflessness. It leads, in other words, to the *imitation* of God—or the striving for *image and likeness.*

What follows is given with caveats. As a practice The Prayer of the Heart is specifically designed for Eastern Orthodox Christians, though it has its parallels in other denominations and paths. If you take it on as a practice, know that it will initiate and draw to you a series of events. For this reason I suggest that you seek out spiritual guidance, preferably from a minister or leader in your denomination who can guide you through appropriate spiritual direction. Whether you seek direction or not, you will, if you adopt a prayer practice such as this, begin to feel the desire for it.

The prayer pattern of Eastern Orthodoxy is primarily ritualistic and formal. That is, church services are very structured and most prayer is done in the form of chanting and singing the words of Holy Elders, as handed down through ecclesiastic prayer books. Spontaneous prayer is usually done internally and silently, and not during services. The Prayer of the Heart, on the other hand, is done anywhere and, potentially, all the time, *without ceasing.*

Many different instructions exist for doing this prayer; there is no one, proscribed technique. Technique, though necessary, can become a stumbling block. This is, after all, called The Prayer of the Heart. As Russian Orthodox Bishop Kallistos Ware points out, "There are no fixed or unvarying rules, necessarily, imposed on all who seek to pray; and equally, there is no mechanical technique, whether physical or mental, which can compel God to manifest his presence. His grace is conferred always as a free gift, and cannot be gained automatically by any method or technique."

100

Unless one is under the guidance of a spiritual director most instructions suggest initially approaching The Jesus Prayer—*Lord Jesus Christ, Son of God, have mercy on me, a sinner*—as a meditation to be performed two or three times a day for a period of fifteen to thirty minutes. As with many prayer and meditation practices it is preferable to choose the same time and place daily; consistency strengthens the prayer pattern.

There is a difference of opinion regarding breathing techniques. Some instructions recommend breathing in on *"Lord Jesus Christ, Son of God,"* and exhaling on *"have mercy on me, a sinner."* The steadiness of a breathing pattern creates a rhythm that helps one relax. On the other hand, some instructors caution against relying on such a pattern because it shifts the emphasis away from the relationship and focuses too much on technique.

Here is a method of meditation that I have used for a number of years. The first part is for relaxation and receptivity, like tilling and preparing the soil. The second part is like planting the seed:

Sit in a comfortable position with the spine straight (this keeps the mind alert and helps prevent falling asleep). You may choose to read this into a tape recorder and let your own voice be an external guide, talking you through the relaxation portion.

Concentrate on and visualize your feet, and feel them with your mind. Gradually move your attention up your body, becoming aware of your legs, then your thighs, then your midsection and chest, then through the fingertips and up the arms, through the shoulders and neck and then the face and skull. Begin again at your feet and mentally feel your muscles and your blood pulsing through your veins and arteries. Work your attention up your body in this way to your head. Start at your feet again and this time feel the places where your skin makes contact with your clothes or the air. Also become aware of sounds and try to hear them as pure sound, as vibration, rather than trying to identify them. Feel the sound with your skin rather than hearing it with your ears.

Imagine a ball of light radiating from your solar plexus, filling your body and visualizing a circle of light all around you. Expand out, allowing the light to fill the room, imagining your body expanding with the light, brushing up against the walls and ceiling as if you have been blown up like a balloon. All the while, concentrate on yourself as the light at the center of the circle, radiating out to fill the room with your presence. Become aware of sounds and the feel of the room, not thinking but feeling. When you have filled the room, or even the entire building with your presence, expanding yourself but always aware of yourself at the center, begin repeating to yourself The Jesus Prayer—*Lord Jesus Christ, Son of God, have mercy on me, a sinner.* Let the prayer radiate from the center, filling your entire, expanded body, and then release it to radiate out into the world. Visualize the words spreading out like ripples on a lake, until they disappear into the universe, to be heard by God. Whenever your mind wanders, just begin reciting again *Lord Jesus Christ, Son of God, have mercy on me, a sinner.* Do this for ten to fifteen minutes, two or three times a day, until you have guidance from your spiritual director to recite it constantly, without ceasing.

Integrating the many facets of our life into unified and focused prayers requires a certain amount of stillness and peace. Since most of us live, work, and breathe in a world full of activity, it is important from time to time, regularly and at fixed times if possible, to bring the mind and heart together in either a focused prayer or in focused quiet: *When the heart has acquired stillness it will perceive the heights and depths of knowledge; and the ear of the still intellect will be made to hear marvellous things from God* (Saint Hesychios the Priest, "On Watchfulness and Holiness," no. 132, *The Philokalia*, vol. I.)

The Prayer of the Heart is not the same as the mantra used in Transcendental Meditation, though it may seem to run a parallel course. In TM, the focus is on deep relaxation, unstressing, and personal benefits for the meditator. The mantra intentionally has no linguistic meaning; it is a sound designed to take one beyond thought. One who practices The Jesus Prayer may experience some of the same physiological benefits but the intent is to deepen the personal relationship with Jesus as Lord and to foster the acquisition of virtue and communion with the Holy Spirit. It is but one of an array of spiritual practices in which a serious Orthodox pilgrim engages. Other prescribed practices include fasting, almsgiving, and daily worship.

To draw an athletic analogy, in high school many of us would walk around with a small blue rubber ball, squeezing it throughout the day to build up hand strength. This strength did not guarantee that we would make our foul shots or pin our opponents, but it complemented the more structured practice sessions where other exercises and repetitions were given by the coaches. The Jesus Prayer is like squeezing that ball. It sets a general prayer pattern into motion that draws other spiritual growth opportunities into our lives. It also concisely reminds us and reinforces what our deepest yearning and intent is.

In *The Way of the Pilgrim* the pilgrim reaches the point, after much practice, where the prayer is so fully integrated into his consciousness that it is as if it prayed itself. The pilgrim's hope is that the mind enters into his heart, causing him to become the prayer in addition to the one doing the prayer. This is a wonderful image and goal but we should realize that this fulfillment came to the hero of *The Way of the Pilgrim* only after he submitted himself to a holy elder and spent many years carrying out the obediences assigned. Prayer in this manner is like chiseling at hard granite, gradually revealing the perfect form that lies in potential within the stone. Change is sometimes subtle, sometimes dramatic. If we reflect upon daily events and keep journals of our lives it is possible to track the gradual changes, the growth, the various major and minor initiations that are drawn to us, to chart our soul's deepening. As the mind enters the heart, without our awareness, a gradual shifting from a materialistic to a mystical view of creation begins to emerge. Meaningfulness is met, but not in the way we expected it. It is never in the way we expect.

Once it is awakened our soul, to a greater extent than we probably realize, has its own prayer constantly pulsing, petitioning for reunion with God. This silent prayer of the human heart, the seat of the soul, brings about its own results as it infiltrates the prayers of our minds. Our most effectual conscious prayers are the ones that align themselves to the yearnings of our inner being. This is why we often receive answers to our prayers that seem to be not exactly what we want but probably exactly what we need. The heart always overrides the mind.

When I lived in a community of twenty-five people at our order's retreat center in Forestville, we decided one day that we wanted a dog. The problem was that everybody had a different idea of what kind of dog. One person, who had grown up with black Labrador retrievers, suggested that they make the best people dogs. Another person wanted a German shepherd, another a collie. We had at least six different strong and many more mild or ambivalent opinions. The meeting ended without consensus. A few weeks later a funny-looking dog walked onto the property, plopped down in front of our kitchen, and adopted us. He was a true mutt, with enough pit bull in him to cause many of us to doubt whether we ought to keep him or give him to the pound. We called another community meeting and debated for hours. One person suggested that Oscar, as he became known, was simply the result of our combined prayer, a little bit of this and a little bit of that. That, of course, did not explain the pit bull aspect except it did have us conclude that maybe God was having some fun with us, shattering all our concepts and expectations. Needless to say, Oscar became part of the community, living at the retreat center with us for a number of years and now living with one of the families who moved off the property into their own home. When he was a bad doggie, which he was at times, we referred to him as an example of the importance of specificity, and a tangible reminder of the old saying, be careful what you ask for, you just might get it. The image of Mick Jagger hovers over the entire episode, mockingly singing, ". . . but you get what you need . . ."

Since we pray without ceasing with every thought, whether we know it or not, we might as well get good at it. Our thoughts manifest in unexpected ways, but they reveal themselves over time as a portrait of our inner lives. When our actions and choices do not reflect our inner prayers and hopes we have conflict, usually manifesting as anxiety and confusion.

The breakthrough at this stage of the journey, the initiation, is the merging of the inner and outer, resulting in a harmonious sense of inner peace. Whether it be as a zen-like acceptance of what is, or a more western approach of proactive strategic religious planning, or as a mystical abandonment to Divine providence, this stage of our journey, like the individual balls of dough waiting to be shaped, is marked by a peace that passes all understanding. We are connecting, aligning, not only with an outer God, but with the God who dwells within. It is at this juncture that the intent of the monastic vocation applies to us all: We are each a soul, alone with God.

―――――――

Soft Thanksgiving Dinner Rolls

One of the most joyous food memories that people have are of warm, soft dinner rolls, slathered in butter, often served at holiday times like Thanksgiving. Warm bread, especially when made into rolls, is the perfect comfort food, linking us to hearth and home and childhood memories. Psychologists report that the smell of fresh-baked bread can be an antidote for depression, and that makes sense to me.

This recipe is perfect for Thanksgiving but is also a wonderful comfort during any time of the year as well. The rolls should be plump, soft, and just slightly sweet. Serve these rolls to your children. The mere thought of them will serve as a strong family memory for years to come, bonding you together whenever anyone smells freshly baked bread.

Mise en Place

Makes I dozen
3 $^1/_2$ *cups unbleached bread or all-purpose flour*
$^1/_4$ *cup wheat bran or wheat germ*
1 $^1/_2$ *teasoons salt* (2 $^1/_2$ teaspoons if using kosher salt)

I *tablespoon instant yeast* (or I $^1/_4$ tablespoons active dry yeast
   dissolved in $^1/_4$ cup lukewarm milk)
$^1/_2$ *cup cooked brown rice or wild rice* (especially at Thanksgiving
   time)
I *cup buttermilk* (or whole milk, or plain yogurt), *lukewarm*
2 *tablespoons honey*
4 *tablespoons butter, melted* (or vegetable oil)
I *egg, well-beaten* (for egg wash)
Poppy or sesame seeds for the tops (optional)

Mixing and Primary Fermentation

Mix all the dry ingredients together, including the cooked
brown or wild rice, in a large bowl. Add the liquid ingredients, except the egg wash, stirring with a large spoon until a
ball of dough is formed. Add more milk if necessary to
gather all the dry ingredients into the ball, making a soft
dough. If the dough is too sticky you can adjust it during the
kneading by adding more flour. Turn the dough onto a lightly
floured work surface and knead for about 10 minutes. The
dough should be soft and pliable, tacky but not sticky. Add
more flour if the dough is too sticky, or dribble in more milk
if the dough is too stiff. When the dough passes the window-
pane test (page 40) place it in a lightly oiled bowl, cover with
a damp towel or plastic wrap, and allow to ferment at room
temperature for approximately 60 minutes, or until the
dough doubles in size.

Punching Down, Weighing,
Rounding, Resting, and Shaping

Turn the dough out onto the counter and divide it into 12
equal pieces (approximately 2 ounces each). Wipe the work

surface clean with a damp (but not wet) cloth and take the pieces, I at a time or I in each hand, and press into the counter. Cup your hand, or hands, curling your fingers slightly, and use the inside pinky edge of the hand to steer the dough in a circular motion, driving the dough down and into the cup of your hand as you continue the circular motion. It should take only a few seconds to round the dough into perfect little balls, with a dimple on the bottom of each. Pinch the dimple closed and place all the rolls on a sheet pan that has been covered with baking parchment. Allow about I or 2 inches between the rolls. Brush the rolls with the egg wash, taking care to coat them evenly. Place the pan in a plastic bag and allow the rolls to proof for approximately I hour, or until doubled in size.

Baking, Cooling, and/or Eating and Storing

Preheat the oven to 400 degrees (350 degrees if convection). Gently brush egg wash on the rolls a second time. Sprinkle on the poppy or sesame seeds, if using. Bake the rolls for about I0 to I2 minutes, or until they are a rich golden brown. Cool the rolls for I0 minutes before serving them. If storing, wait until the rolls are completely cool and double-wrap them in plastic wrap. Store in a cool, dark place or freeze (they will keep for up to 6 months in the freezer).

7

Surrendering to Synergy

The eye by which I see God is the same eye by which God sees me. My eye and God's eye are one and the same. God cannot know Himself without me.

Meister Eckart

During the time I spent at the Forestville Retreat Center I held many jobs. Like the Karate Kid, who received training without knowing it by washing cars and painting fences, the day-to-day tasks of working on the property were as much a part of my training as theological study and daily prayer life. During the five years prior to opening Brother Juniper's Café and Bakery I spent time in our candle shop, tending the bees, working in the garden, turning the compost piles, helping out in the kitchen, washing cars, patching potholes in the roads, and doing any other task to which I was assigned. It didn't take long for the property manager to realize how limited my carpentry and mechanical skills were, so I tended to get the jobs requiring less skill, the menial tasks, the utterly boring jobs. Part of me loved these assignments and part of me was anxious for more opportunities to work in ministry with people. My real struggle was focusing on what was happening in the moment rather than on what I thought was around the corner. But from these years of training and soul formation I slowly came to understand what is now a governing life lesson: *Stay focused on what is in front of you and the rest will come.*

Whenever I worried about fulfilling what I thought of as "my destiny," I ended up full of anxiety and lost the focus of the moment. The fear of being thwarted is a deeply rooted gremlin. I'd known for years that a key to spiritual practice is the ability to stay focused in the moment; every path and discipline stresses it. I used to think that meditating and doing concentration exercises would be how I'd learn this, and they certainly helped and started a process in motion. But the way I really learned it was by being thrust in a situation where my commitment to the principle of patience and long-suffering was really tested.

The five years at the center led to another seven years of creating first a restaurant and then a bakery business. Brother Juniper's Café and Bakery was both the most amazing and difficult challenge of my life. I cannot recall the number of times, after particularly grueling days, that Susan or I would ask each other, why are we doing this instead of something else? Most of the time, after working it through, we'd come to the conclusion that we needed to complete what was in front of us before the next thing would be revealed. We knew there had to be meaning in it even if we could not be sure what that meaning was or where it would lead. We trusted or learned to trust through our prayers and the support of others in our community and our families that there really would be a next step and that we would recognize it when we were there and would know what to do.

Our original idea for Brother Juniper's was to create a small showcase café for some of the food products Susan and I had developed, with the hope that some of them might spin off into cottage industries that other members of our community could run. We were looking for sustainable livelihoods for our members and thought it might come from food products. The first year was particularly grueling, going in to work at 8 A.M. in order to be open for lunch by 11 A.M. and not getting back to our cabin high on the hill of the retreat center property until about 10:30 P.M. We gradually built up a loyal following and were on the verge of breaking through to our first really big day when the *Santa Rosa Press Democrat*, the daily paper of Sonoma County, did a cover story on us. It focused especially on how a percentage of our income was used to help support a homeless shelter, Raphael House, operated by our order in San Francisco. The next day, we knew, promised to bring in a big crowd, and it did. As much as we tried to be ready for it the response was so overwhelming that we spent the entire day turning out plate after plate, passing out complimentary glasses of ginger fizz to the waiting lines of people, and just barely maintaining our sanity. By the time we closed we were so exhausted we thought we might have to lock the doors, go home to sleep, and come back in the middle of the night to clean up the thoroughly decimated kitchen and dining room. As we sat in the café with our few helpers, catching our breath and just soaking up the implications of the day, we heard the sound of live music out on the street, getting louder as it seemed to be approaching. Before we knew it, a small marching band of about ten people, led by the musicians from our community, Br. Robert DeLucia and Br. Fred Doubleday, entered the café playing "When the Saints Go Marching In." After a few more songs everyone jumped into clean-up mode and blitz-cleaned the café in forty-five minutes, restoring it to a crisp sparkle as if there had never been a record-breaking day.

This was the yin and yang of running a business; the joy of feeding people and building relationships, the deep fatigue squeezing every ounce of energy from our weary bones. It was relentless, taking a major turn when on Christmas morning, nearly two years into the project, Susan's back gave way while simply opening her Christmas presents, herniating two discs. We had already begun building our new bakery facility with the plan of me running the bakery while Susan ran the café. That all changed, as she now faced a long recuperation. Fortunately, a number of people from our community stepped into the breach and helped keep Brother Juniper's afloat, along with some very reliable employees. We managed to keep the café/restaurant going for another year while I focused on the bakery (sometimes splitting myself between the two locations), until it became clear that the bakery should become the primary focus. We reluctantly closed the restaurant, despite the petitions of the local populace, and faced the next challenge in front of us, building the bakery into a successful business. Four years later, when the time came to sell Brother Juniper's Bakery, we knew we had done all that we could with it and it was finally time to move on to the next adventure. It was as if the escalator rose to meet our feet. By that time we were physically, mentally, and spiritually spent, our egos squeezed, stretched, and wrung out like fresh wash.

You hear a lot of talk in the spiritual life about losing the ego, trancending the ego, or becoming ego-less. We probably all have different ideas of what that means, but I think any idea of losing the ego is terribly misleading. I can live with the idea of overcoming enslavement to our passions, or getting free from attachment to the things of this world, but there's no way any of us can healthily lose our egos and still accomplish anything. Overcoming ego has mostly to do with humility and submission to God's will, of a striving for purity and virtue that actually strengthens the ego. It is learning to work cooperatively with God, amalgamating our human will with God's will. To do this effectively requires humility and, oddly, a strong healthy ego. During the Brother Juniper's years we experienced our egos getting an intense workout, including a number of buildups and an equal number of punch-downs. However, the real lesson in all of this was learning how to dance cooperatively with God, which often is as much a matter of patience as it is of action.

This is the sacred relationship we've been calling *synergy,* in which human effort meets the will of God and transformation takes place. One of the virtues that every seeker needs to develop at some point along the way is patience or, in religious vernacular, *waiting on the Lord.* Practicing the virtue of patience is just one way our egos learn to wait upon the will of God, but it is part of the process towards a deep and ultimate goal: being at peace. Finding the *peace that passes all understanding* is easier said than done, but understanding it in light of patience is actually initiatory. What makes it initiatory is the surrender, relaxing into the reality of synergy as a governing principle in our theostic journey.

When I get to the stage of bread production called *benching,* I often talk about this principle of patience with my students. Benching, or resting dough, is also about patiently waiting. It seems as if nothing is happening, the round pieces of raw dough just sit on the bench, the gluten relaxing. But this step is an important prelude to the next stage, called *shaping.* In many bakeries there are large machines, built with hundreds of soft canvas pockets, that actually pass uniform balls of dough from pocket to pocket for about fifteen minutes before discharging them to a molding machine, where they are shaped into loaves. While the primary purpose of this rest period is to allow the gluten to relax so the dough can be extended into longer shapes, fermentation and flavor development is occurring as well. There is more going on than meets the eye. It's kind of similar to taking a deep breath before shooting a foul shot. It relieves anxiety and, in a way, allows the *ego* of the bread, its identity, to relax into the will of the bread maker so it can be properly shaped into its final form.

It is at the parallel stage of the human journey, in the midst of that deep breath, that we grapple with the relationship between effort and grace. Having surrendered, so to speak, to the unfolding of Divine providence, we are also compelled to work harder in our striving for virtue. Both our inner and outer lives are deepening, the outer adventures reflecting the fruits of our inner explorations. We are enjoying the relaxation and lifting of anxiety as we develop patience and other virtues, but this inner work inevitably creates accountability and corresponding outer work. We may be in retreat from the world but the world never really goes away—we just learn to manage ourselves better in it as we grow in our understanding of the synergy between our efforts and grace.

Somewhere along the way I learned that the word *synergy* had a deeper meaning than any corporation glibly using it in strategic planning sessions could possibly imagine. Centuries before Buckminster Fuller made the word popular and consultants made it part of business vocabularies, it was adopted as a guiding principle by the early Christian Church, resolving the question that haunts so many Christians even today: Is a person saved by faith or works? The synergistic answer is by both, working together cooperatively.

When Meister Eckhart, the famous Catholic mystic, took this principle to its furthest extension in saying *the eye by which I see God is the same eye by which God sees me. My eye and God's eye are one and the same. God cannot know Himself without me,* his experience came from a very personal theostic vision, pushing synergy to its limits as a guiding principle and inspiring us, hopefully, to make it a compelling force in our lives.

Pragmatically, the problem with mystical experience is that it is an unearned gift. On the other hand, the problem with ascetic labors, works, or personal effort is that effort does not guarantee mystical experience. However, from the perspective of sacred psychology, synergy provides a metaphysical principle that envelopes both method and experience.

The theostic goal for us, then, is the same realization Saint Symeon the New Theologian had when, in the tenth century, he heard the voice of God tell him, "*Yes, I am God, the one who became man for your sake. And behold, I have created you, as you see, and I shall make you God*" (p. 224). This is the crux of the mystical journey of the soul: *and I shall make you God.* How much of that, I wonder, is being transmitted in churches today? And how many of us grasp that this is where ultimate meaning is found, found within the arena of each of our own religious traditions as they lead us inward to that ultimate reality, . . . *and I shall make you God.*

It is important in dealing with concepts of such mystical magnitude to understand more fully the relationship between the mystical and ascetic experience. In *ascesis* (ascetic labors of purification), an important part of the methodology of traditional Christianity, the acquisition of virtue is a result of personal effort, *praxis* (practice), which is then *synergistically* boosted by the general grace that God grants to all who strive. A mystic, on the other hand, is one in whom the *spiritual gifts of the Holy Spirit* predominate over human efforts; grace-infused insight takes precedence over acquired virtues. In the mystical life then, the soul receives, for whatever reason, a blessing in excess and even out of proportion to any striving. A metaphor often used to describe the difference between the mystic and ascetic polarities is the example of rowing a boat versus sailing it. The oar represents the ascetic effort while the sail is the mystical receptivity that unfurls to catch the wind. The traditional orthodox view of this is that the mystic and ascetic paths are intimately intertwined and mutually supportive. Ascetic struggle tempers mystical fervor and mystical grace infuses joyful ecstasy into ascetic labors.

A friend once told me that when he worked as an automobile salesman there were code words to describe different kinds of customers, like "window shoppers" or "negotiators." His favorite was what he called a "do me." This was someone who came in determined to leave with a car, regardless of price, and just put himself in the salesman's hands. This passive trust can be viewed as either admirable or foolish, but given the nature of the automobile business it probably means not getting the best possible price, though it also means leaving in a new car. The trade-off is that "do me" people have a ready-made excuse when things do not go their way; it is always somebody else's fault, even God's.

Waiting on the Lord does not mean we wake up each day saying, "Okay God, do me and I'll go along for the ride." Synergy releases us from the false notion that to be spiritual means to simply be passive. In fact, it demands we be co-active, but it is in patience, and the developing of virtue in general, that we make the effort to recognize the difference between our personal will and God's will. Since we are created in the image and likeness of God we have a responsibility to develop and purify our wills; we make decisions throughout every day for which we need to take responsibility. Virtue, being the energy of God, is not just something we do but is something into which we tap. We practice virtue so that, we hope, virtue will flow through us. When that happens, we approach the threshold of theosis.

A number of years ago I was going through one of those dark times when everything seemed hopeless. I had just botched an important fund-raising assignment costing us thousands of dollars in relief money for Cambodia, lost a relationship I thought was headed towards marriage, and faced reassignment. These dark nights of the soul are, we all know, necessary and crucial to spiritual growth, but believing it and living it are very different. Desperation would not really be desperate if it could be simply thought away with an aphorism, as if it were but a mosquito. There is not much growth when the solution is as simple as saying, "I don't want to be despondent anymore, so there, I'm not" (though this does work at times).

No, this was a tough period in which my entire life and personality was up for internal personal review. I had no confidence, every choice I made seemed to be the wrong one, and I was overwhelmed with shame at the degree of my inadequacies. Looking back it is easier now to appreciate how important that time was because it brought me, literally, to my knees. After some deep soul-searching, I found myself at the altar rail in an empty chapel, sobbing in a private confession with God, whom I felt I had betrayed and abandoned. Then, unexpectedly, I had one of those epiphanatic moments in the presence of an all-forgiving Father, the one I had dreamed about for years. It was different from the Highway 80 awakening, but it was also a renewal of it, taken to a much higher level. I experienced a wave of unconditional love and forgiveness, not for the first time, but in a new, deeper, and all-encompassing way. The weight of my sorrows disappeared, physically lifted from me, and I sensed that through an act of supernatural love virtue was flowing through me. I was being given a fresh start, an initiation, yet another rebirth within a life of rebirths. I started sobbing uncontrollably, a cleansing, purging kind of crying, and I left the chapel knowing that something had changed in me. There were no solutions revealed that night, but despair had been replaced by a sober hope, a weight had been removed. It was a pure unearned gift. Inwardly, I celebrated life for the first time in many months, yet still wondered if I would ever really live joyfully, confidently, and vibrantly again.

The next day a friend asked me if I would be willing to help out in a talent show fund-raiser. It was to be a spaghetti dinner followed by a musical show. She wanted me to do an opening presentation about the spaghetti harvest. I couldn't believe it; I was being asked to do a comedy routine! At first I hesitated but finally agreed and came up with a sketch in which I pretended to be showing the audience a slide show (a gimmick made popular by the comic Jackie Vernon many years ago) about workers in the imaginary town of Pastafajool, Italy, gathering the strands of ripe spaghetti from the spaghetti vines, replete with historic commentary and human interest stories about some of the people of Pastafajool. While rehearsing with the other performers I learned they needed someone for a few songs, so I volunteered for those and before long I had a substantial role in the program, singing from *Guys and Dolls* and *Godspell.* The event was a big success. Even now, many years later, we still reminisce about the infamous spaghetti dinner. It has become one of those landmark events that tap into legendary status and become part of our personal folklore.

I think of the talent show event as the post-initiatic payoff, an extension of my earlier chapel experience, enabling me not only to break out of my despair but also to springboard into a brand new cycle of vibrant activity and application of the things I had learned during my crisis. It is hard for me to recall that period of my life without experiencing emotions of joy and appreciation, mingled with bittersweet melancholy, for an initiation is always accompanied by the pain of growth. I once interviewed Robert Bly on the subject of initiations for *Epiphany Journal.* He referred to the example of a tribal elder knocking out the tooth of a brave young initiate so that the youth would never forget the significance of that moment. "There is," he said, "always a corresponding physical event, usually painful."

Well, I still have all of my teeth but I will never forget the night I felt God's virtue flow into me. As in other events, my life was unalterably changed that night in a way that has carried me through

many subsequent crises. It was, much as on Mount Shasta, a deepening of the knowledge, by direct experience, of God's unconditional love. I worked hard for that experience. I'd never dug so
deep into the darkness of my being as I did during the days leading up to that moment, so as I think back upon it I can honestly
say I worked for it. But when it came I instantly knew how unwor-
thy I was, how much it was pure gift. That was more than twenty
years ago, and I now recognize it as pure synergy. From that moment to this my dance with God changed me in a way clearly at-
tributable to that moment. That is how I know it was an initiation.

The English theologian John Henry Newman said, *"It is very
hard for anyone to believe something he cannot first imagine to be true."*

Two exemplars of the mystical, theostic tradition in Eastern
Christianity were Symeon the New Theologian and Gregory
Palamas. They, as deeply as any teachers or writers in the history of
Christian mystical theology, outlined the method and practice that
lead one to union with God. Church history has provided a long
list of great mystics, whether Protestant, Catholic, or Orthodox
and each has their champions. But it was Symeon and Gregory
Palamas who definitively articulated the reality of the theostic possibility into the Christian faith. For this they endure as true hero
figures, the good guys, within the historical paradoxes of a religious
tradition that has spawned both good and bad memories.

When Symeon the New Theologian and, later, Gregory
Palamas fought for acceptance of the mystic/ascetic alliance in
the eleventh and twelfth centuries, they brought the first mille-
nium of Christianity to a stunning theological synthesis. They are
the two men most identified with the roots of hesychasm, the way
of quiet (Quietism), and the emergence of The Jesus Prayer. Their
teachings became for the east, along with Thomas Aquinas's
Scholasticism in the west, the major influences of Christian mystical theology during the past thousand years.

Symeon (949–1022), who was given the honorific The New Theologian in tribute to his ability to synthesize previous mystical theology into a new articulation, led the way. He showed that it is indeed possible to have a direct and personal experience of what he called the Uncreated Light of God. Though his first taste of this, as a young man, was as an unearned mystical gift, he then dedicated his life to ascetic monastic discipline in order to prepare himself for continued experience and to teach others. From Luke 18 he borrowed The Publican's Prayer, "Lord Jesus Christ, have mercy upon me," as a means to recover his moment of revelation and taught others to pray in the same manner.

His message was furthered two centuries later by Gregory Palamas (1296–1359), the Archbishop of Salonika, a more systematic thinker who formulated a theological explanation for the mystical possibility and formalized a spiritual practice, which included The Jesus Prayer, as a means to its attainment. He never articulated a logical answer to the riddle how can God be both immanent and transcendent but asserted the paradox: We attain to participation in the divine nature, and yet at the same time it remains totally inaccessible. We need to affirm both at the same time and to preserve the antimony as a criterion for right doctrine.

Condescension is a recurrent theme in mystical theology, indicating our total dependency upon the Supreme First Principle, a transcendent Creator God who *chooses* to incarnate through humanity. With this first mystery as a starting point, all theory and practice has as its final aim the personal realization of this Creator. So while the realization of God cannot be earned by effort alone, we have a much better shot at it if we do everything within our power to bring it about.

Saints Symeon and Palamas made it clear that their notion of deification, or theosis, was based on an experience of the *energy* of God, not the *essence*. This preserved the transcendent, unknowable quality of God while yet rendering Him knowable by his radiance. Symeon was careful to distinguish between this phenomenon of the vision of light and its impact on our consciousness. The goal, as Basil Krivocheine explains it in his study of Symeon, was "*. . . a personal encounter with Christ manifesting Himself through light and communion with Him. Furthermore, it is only when Christ begins to speak in our own heart through His Holy Spirit that we acquire personal knowledge about Him. A simple vision of light does not bestow this; on the contrary, it can cause an immense lassitude, a profound mystical dissatisfaction*" (pp. 24–25).

Symeon's teaching to his followers, as Karen Armstrong describes in *A History of God*, was to seek out not merely a vision but a "transfiguring reality in their own souls." Phenomena is only useful if it leads to spiritual growth.

121

In my years of God-seeking I witnessed in others and participated in many motives and objectives. Phenomena such as auras and psychic powers drew me in the early years; personal power was a compelling hook for a time and a season; charisma, that enigmatic something that someone else had and everyone else wanted, was another. As the gates narrowed and the energies of virtue condescended to trickle into this world and form me, I came to realize that all those alluring, compelling early goals had brought me to a desire for a transfiguring reality in my soul. Empowerment, the hook that drew me in, gave way to the power of patience, and the power of the present moment. The payoff, I learned, is not in out-of-this-world phenomenological experiences but in experiencing the out-of-this-world quality of each moment.

When I greet a new group of students on their first day of my bread-making class, I tell them that I expect them to bring 100 percent of themselves to the workbench, and I promise to meet them with 100 percent of myself. Between their efforts and my teaching we can make culinary magic. When I ask my students to bring all of themselves to the bench, what I am really asking them to do is to trust me, to place themselves in my hands and to allow me to lead them to the promised land of world-class bread. The most important part of my job is creating an environment in which the students feel safe enough to make that leap of faith. I bring every bit of credibility I have ever earned to the bench; I bring my knowledge, my experience, my skill. But the singlemost important thing the students want from me, and every teacher, is to know that we are vitally concerned with their success. When I am able to convey that to them they are able to let go, to relax the way gluten relaxes in a piece of rounded dough when it is given time to bench. The relaxed dough becomes putty in the hands of a skilled baker; the dough surrenders itself to be well handled, to be shaped into its final form.

The spiritual empowerment I seek at this stage of my journey comes from surrendering into the synergistic process, doing everything possible to bring 100 percent of myself into the needs of the moment, knowing that this effort will be met by the energy, or virtue, of God. To do that I too have to relax, to let go and, most importantly, trust. Surrendering into synergy is not simply a recognition of the concept. It is an action that is simultaneously both active and passive, aggressive and receptive. Surrendering into synergy is a major breakthrough in the spiritual journey for it allows us to be used as both a receiver and a transmitter of the energy we receive; it allows us to enter the royal interior priesthood.

8

Tempering the Soul

During my young seminary days in San Francisco, I used to get away whenever I could and hike on Mount Tamalpais, we call it Mt. Tam, a small mountain and regional park just north of the city, just past the Golden Gate Bridge in Marin County. Sometimes I would take a pup tent and camp out there, using the campground as a debarkation point for day hikes through either John Muir Woods, a spectacular redwood preserve on the lower slope, or I'd head upwards onto the scenic Crest Trail overlooking Stinson Beach and the Pacific Ocean. Either direction was glorious but they evoked different self-reflection qualities, so I would intuitively choose according to my need. I'd go down into the woods when I needed to grapple with my spiritual struggles and inner life, to face my sins, demons, and inadequacies. I'd take the high trail when I needed to strategize about a course of action. I did not plan it that way or figure out which path enhanced which process but only realized long afterwards in retrospection how each path affected me and how my intuition guided my choice.

Whether living a vowed life in a formal spiritual community, or simply a life of personal striving in the world at large, we all face necessary times of aloneness, deep aloneness, that must be endured in order to grow into who we are meant to be. I remember spending an entire weekend on Mt. Tam just grappling with the question: Am I lonely or just alone? For me, at that particular time, this was an important issue in my psychological well being, and I was not interested in stock answers; I needed to arrive at my own conclusions. The real issue was coming to grips with the reality of being a soul alone with God. Once I accepted the inescapability and whyness of that it was much easier to endure whatever loneliness I might feel from time to time. In fact, when I at last realized the necessity of that aloneness it so dwarfed the loneliness that for the first time in my life I was no longer afraid to be alone. I had a why to endure the how.

124

My walks through the redwoods of John Muir Park were especially memorable because they caused me to feel emotions and internal depths of my being that became sense memories in much the same way that certain foods become flavor memories. Even now a walk in the woods triggers remembrances, linking me back not only to previous walks but also to the feelings and thoughts those walks evoked. There is something special about the shadows and streams of light that filter through the woods, triggering moods and unleashing sensitivities. The overall effect is to drive me deep within myself, yet be hypersensitive to the smell of bark and soil, the sound of bugs and lizards, slight subtle movements of branches or leaves, and the tickle of leaves and ladybugs as they brush against my skin. I realize at some point along the way how utterly alone I am (even when hiking with someone else, as I've often done) and how much I am an individual no matter how much I think I am linked to everyone and all of creation. These kinds of thoughts make you take yourself seriously, significantly so, while being acutely aware of your simultaneous insignificance, your puniness in the great scheme of things. No matter how you play it, relating to yourself as significant or insignificant, the paradox sucks you in, either railing against or submitting to the reality that you inescapably see. Eventually, if you hang in there long enough and just keep walking, you find your way out of the woods and back to base camp. I worked out much of my angst in Muir Woods, wrestled with both angels and demons, and developed an appreciation for self-reflection that I still value even though I rarely get to the woods anymore. In recent times I've had to find my soulfulness, to connect with that realm of sensitivity, without the trigger of the woods and its sensory trip switches, but through other meditative practices. The monks call it, metaphorically, living in the desert, but for me the metaphor is a purposeful walk through the woods.

I recently revisited the Forestville Retreat Center, where I lived for seven years, often walking the woods of mostly oak and pine with a few redwoods scattered here and there. It is now a full-fledged monastery. During the day's visit I spent time with an old friend who is a monk there and was amazed at how just a brief exposure to the property, just seeing some of those trees and dirt pathways that I haven't walked in over ten years, could trigger so many feelings that connect me to my past, true to the paradoxical question of how can I be both significant and insignificant? Being there reminded me again of both the importance of my being and my utter inconsequentiality in the greater scheme of things. Living between these paradoxical points provides an interesting framework for how to conceptualize myself in relation to my Creator, through the many tests that temper my soul as a channel for grace to flow into this world.

I realized, as the waves of emotion and the reflective mood kicked in, how much I missed these dips into the inner me found in the woods. The memories of plunging through Muir Woods or the woods of Forestville and the tangle of my psyche, working at untangling in a desperate act of self understanding in pursuit of meaningfulness, are planted deep within as signposts of my unfolding.

I was recently in a church not my own, standing in the back of a small chapel while on a rare Sunday visit to San Francisco. I observed a woman who spent a great deal of time on her knees praying at the Mary Shrine. It was clear she was struggling with a deep concern and was petitioning Mary, The Blessed Mother (often referred to in Orthodoxy as the Theotokos, or God-bearer), for intervention. There was a sense of desperation in her praying, an intensity and earnestness that pricked my conscience. I don't know if it was because it was not my regular house of worship, where I have grown used to the people around me, but so much passion emanated from her that it caused me to realize how long it had been since I felt that kind of desperation, enough to drive me to my knees or send me into the woods in a life or death search for truth. I recalled how important desperation is and has been in my life, how it leads to fervent prayers. Usually I avoid desperation even though I know that when I am content and feeling pretty good about myself, my prayers are less fervent. I wait for desperation to find me rather than seek it out. The woman's desperation alerted me to a growing complacency in my striving.

Some people are good at keeping the pressure on themselves. They are naturally self-disciplined while I know that I need strong external structure, daily patterns of living and spiritual practice, to keep me in touch with the parameters of my crucible, to remind me during the good times that the underlying sense of purpose that gives my life meaning and drives my will to fulfillment is when I am being a channel for grace. I forget this unless I stay in the battlefield of unseen warfare, which for me is the willingness to balance my life in this world of activity with an inner life of such utter aloneness with God that it verges on, but no longer succumbs to, loneliness. But the world of assumptions that must be embraced in order for such an unseen warfare to make sense is a challenge that requires daily renewal. This is where the distinction between the competing worldviews that rage within me comes to a head. The conventional, attractive choice, even among people who practice religion religiously, is to be of this world. The radical, mystical, theostic choice is for other-worldliness. To make this choice means staying in contact with an operational belief in the existence of a heavenly world, of a Supreme Being who is simultaneously impersonal yet deeply and personally involved in my life, both transcendent and immanent. It means connecting with a pantheon of poetic-yet-existent beings, seen and unseen, who mediate for me between these seen and unseen worlds. While many of us profess such a belief system very few actually live as if this were our perceived reality. Even with the compelling epiphanies that defined my life's meaning and direction, I rarely fight hard enough to keep this mystical reality alive and in the forefront. For that I need help, both structurally and in the form of people who can mediate for me when I am not sharp enough to mediate for myself.

The struggle between these two worldviews, being of this world versus being not of this world, has been described in many metaphorical terms and images throughout the ages, such as the idea of the fall and redemption of mankind. The way I understand it is that the fallen nature represents the conventional human state, explained mythopoetically in the Judeo-Christian tradition as a result of Adam's original sin. Through messianic intervention (God made flesh), we are sacrificially freed from this state and redeemed as children of God. Every religion has its own way of working this out. Regardless of the theological differences in articulating this, all religions require a leap of faith somewhere along the line—and then a continuous lifetime of such leaps, renewed again and again. This is difficult in a world in which leaps of faith are less honored than leaps of logic and bottom-line thinking. This series of faith leaps is the true spiritual combat of unseen warfare—an unending battle for reconciliation in the eternal striving of a seemingly divided self in pursuit of an intuited unification, or Self-Realization. This is *theosis*, the bringing together of heaven and earth, and the experience of the peace that passes all understanding. Staying in the battle, keeping your head and heart in the game when the cares of the world are so attractively distracting, this is the initiation of tempering. Tempering confirms our resolve to stay true to the path that has called us, even when we have lost the edge of desperation that got us there in the first place.

The eighth stage of bread making is to dough like the walk in the woods experience is to the soul. The pieces of bulk dough, now divided into individual pieces, rounded and rested, are formed into their final shape and set out for their second and final fermentation, called proofing. We call it proofing to prove that the dough is still alive, that it hasn't used up all its *push*. It now must replicate the growth of the bulk dough, but as a stand-alone loaf. Most of the flavor and character has been developed during the bulk rise, but having been degassed during the various punch downs and shaping steps, the dough has to rise yet one more time before going into the oven, where it undergoes the transformation from raw dough to finished bread.

This final rise sustains the loaf through the final stages, recapitulating the previous stages, the macrocosmic bulk dough, in a microcosmic single loaf. Sustainability is a virtue that many pilgrims overlook when enthusiastically embarking on the spiritual quest. We need nourishment and tools to give us stamina.

One of the most powerful prayers available today is from the Optina Monastery of Russia, home of the last of the great mystic elders of modern times (most of whom were killed in Communist gulags). It describes the ideal state and attitude of the well-tempered soul, and as a daily practice nourishes the compelling vision of the spiritual quest, embodying the principles of sacred psychology within the Judeo-Christian mystical tradition. Susan and I pray this every morning as part of our daily devotions and I find that it is the single most effective daily practice in keeping me connected to my sense of meaning, mission, and purpose.

The Prayer of the Optina Elders

Grant unto me, O Lord, that with peace of mind I may
   face all that this new day is to bring.
Grant unto me to dedicate myself completely to Thy
   Holy Will.
For every hour of this day, instruct and support me in
   all things.
Whatsoever tidings I may receive during the day, do
   Thou teach me to accept tranquilly, in the firm con-
   viction that all eventualities fulfill Thy Holy Will.
Govern Thou my thoughts and feelings in all I do and
   say.
When things unforeseen occur, let me not forget that all
   cometh down from Thee.
Teach me to behave sincerely and rationally toward every
   member of my family, that I may bring confusion and
   sorrow to none.
Bestow upon me, my Lord, strength to endure the fatigue of the day and to bear my part in all its passing
   events.
Amen.

When I stepped out of the strong community structures that formed and supported my soul development, I had to find ways to maintain the growth and keep the desire for a spiritual life strong. Just as I've divided bread production into twelve stages and soul initiations into ten stages as an exercise in connecting the dots of my personal experience to the universals that underlie it, I also turn to the elders of my tradition for correlation. Saint Maximus the Confessor, one of the great Patristic Fathers and mystics of the early church, provides a more general framework around which to understand the journey of a soul, dividing the spiritual life into three stages. ". . . his teaching about a personal approach to salvation is divided into three basic parts: I) 'practical philosophy' or praxis, 2) 'natural theoria' or simply theoria, and 3) 'mystical theology' or simply theology. The first purifies a person of passion and adorns him with virtues; the second illuminates his nous (author's note: the human mind that corresponds with the mind of God) with true knowledge; and the third crowns him with the highest mystical experience, which Saint Maximus calls 'ecstasy.' These three parts constitute the basic stages on the path of man's personal salvation."

My interpretation of this threefold structure is that spiritual practice, theological and philosophical knowledge, and direct experience, or ecstasy (which literally means *out of the body*) are the three pillars of the theostic journey. Spiritual practice is the process of unseen warfare, battling through personal effort and self-discipline against anything that might hinder the flow of God's grace into the world. It is all about virtue because virtue is, by root definition, the energy of God. So the various practices we take on, whether they be devotional, ascetic, or charitable (prayer, fasting, and almsgiving) are exercises in practicing the presence of God, practicing the interior priesthood, practicing living in and as the image and likeness of God. Spiritual practice is about the efforts we bring to the "bench" in order to know God, and about developing, through exercise, the stamina necessary to go to war to overcome or purify any part of us that lacks virtue.

"Spiritual struggles and labours generate gladness in the soul, that is, as the passions have been stilled; for what is difficult for those who are still dominated by the senses is easy and even delightful for an aspiring soul that through its holy exertions has acquired a longing for God and is smitten with desire for divine knowledge."

Natural theoria, or theoretical knowledge, is the study of our tradition, our belief systems, the doctrines, dogmas and credos that help us frame our worldview. It includes spiritual reading, study of history and the lives of saints, and dialogue with fellow pilgrims.

Mystical theology or ecstacy is the personal Divine encounter, the synergy of our efforts and God's gift. In the Eastern Church of which Maximus was a part there was no distinction between the mystical and the theological as there seems to be in our western understanding. Theologia implied knowledge through direct experience rather than through intellectual understanding, as it does today. This is the end result, the final stage of the theostic journey. Considering the price one pays to reach this end, it takes connection with a very compelling vision or experience to keep the motivation vivified. Maintaining contact with this compelling vision is the challenge through which tempering takes us. Tempering is, in fact, the testing and strengthening of our commitment to the vision of our quest.

When we make bread we have enough experience with the end result so that we know what we are shooting for and what to expect at each stage. It is not always so for the spiritual pilgrim unless he or she is well guided and fortified, confirmed in the awakening that began the whole process. Guidance is something we must seek out, but fortification and nourishment also come in many forms. One of the most enriching is meditating and reentering the realm of meaningfulness, connecting again and again with the compelling vision.

I developed a walking meditation for myself many years ago that strengthens my connection to my visions of the past, bringing them into the present. It can be done in the woods, on the crests of hills and mountains, or even on the streets of the city. This practice transforms any place of activity into a place of peace and reflection, leavening all efforts of abandonment to Divine providence into synergistic upliftment and enrichment.

Here's what I do: Before starting out on a walk I take a few deep breaths and relax long enough to center myself and focus just below my heart on the solar plexus. I imagine that there are antennae growing out of this center, picking up signals from God. I usually say a prayer before the walk, either the Prayer of the Optina Elders or a spontaneous prayer asking for similar guidance. Sometimes I invoke my favorite saint or saints and ask for their intercession and protection, and to draw unto me the opportunities I need to grow. Then I let my solar plexus, my heart center, take the lead and draw me forward as I follow the pull of the antennae as if they were a divining rod leading me to water. As I walk I focus my attention straight ahead, not looking around but letting my gaze go where my center leads. It feels like I'm being drawn by a magnet towards my destination. If I have a specific end point in mind I follow the magnetic pull towards it but stay aware of intuitive tugs that lead me to explore other avenues, imagining myself as one of Moses' followers walking through the Red Sea as it parts before my every step. As I walk I sense the energy field around me, acting as a cocoon of protection, but I stay mindful of sounds and people nearby. It's as if I'm gliding towards my destination, weaving my way through the path that unfolds with every step, noticing the people and sites that pass through my peripheral vision. Within minutes my mind has calmed enough for me to start the prayer of the heart. When I first developed this walk, I would silently chant Sat Nam, or my TM mantra (still a secret), but now I pray to God through my Christian voice, knowing and trusting that God will meet and lead me. If thoughts spring up that distract me I don't fight them but instead I just let them drift through me and away, trailing behind me like the wind and the cars or trees or people who pass the opposite way. It is as if I am back on Highway 80, but with a new mantra based on how I presently understand and relate to God. The very act drives me deeper within myself and I begin to feel a radiance, a glow, that goes beyond my senses. I know that this radiance is not only glowing from me but is drawing to me awaiting experiences and opportunities. I am both alert and distant, in the world but not of it, experiencing a peace that is rare, is not based on external events but on just being fully in the present. At some point I become aware of my breathing. Is it labored, smooth, deep, or shallow? I begin to notice that my silent prayers are matching to the "in" breath and the "out" breath as I fall into a natural rhythm, walking, but being gently pulled by God to my destination.

This is but one of many ways to get reconnected and renewed in our vision. We each have ways that work to accomplish this and our various religions have traditional practices that are both individualized and communal. When I joined a local gym and was given my orientation tour the fitness director explained the weights and Nautilus and Cybex and the new fancy computerized equipment in a way that I will never forget, and it changed the way I viewed my workouts. He said, "All these pieces are good, they each work and improve your strength and fitness. But the best ones are the ones you enjoy using, the ones you return to day after day and don't get bored with. The only good equipment here is the equipment you use."

It is the same with spiritual practice. There are so many exercises, so many ways to meditate, contemplate God, and to pray; so many methods and disciplines even within a particular tradition. These methods, though, will not work for us if we don't practice them, and practice them repeatedly. Even more importantly, though, is the fervency of our intent, our desperation for truth, and the connection with the vision that all this exercise is supposed to enliven. Is our heart engaged?

There is a story with many variations, told in every religion but most famously retold by Leo Tolstoy in *The Three Hermits*, in which a powerful and famous bishop visits three hermit monks on an island and, in the course of their discussions, teaches them how to pray the Lord's Prayer. The simple monks have a hard time remembering the exact words but the bishop, imperiously patient, goes over it again and again. Finally, he leaves the island and, while being rowed back to the mainland, pondering the pros and cons of simple piety and congratulating himself for teaching the hermits the proper way to do this prayer, he sees figures in the mist drawing closer. It turns out to be the three monks walking across the water in pursuit of the boat. When they catch it they humbly say to the bishop, "We have forgotten your teaching, servant of God. As long as we kept repeating it we remembered, but when we stopped saying it for a time, a word dropped out, and now it has all gone to pieces. We can remember nothing of it. Teach us again."

"Your own prayer will reach the Lord, men of God. It is not for me to teach you. Pray for us sinners." Then the bishop bowed low before the old men and they turned and walked back across the sea.

Another traditional story, told me by Professor Jacob Needleman when I interviewed him for *Ephiphany Journal* in 1984, makes this point in a different way:

A king exiles his son during some quarrel. After many years, as the king is dying, he wants to turn his kingdom over to his son. He sends couriers out to find him. They look high and low, and after many months of searching, they find the son dancing drunkenly in a tavern. The courier goes up to the son, finally, and says, "Sire, your father the king has forgiven you. You can have anything you want in the kingdom . . . so, what shall I tell the king, your father?" The son stops for a moment, and says, "What I really want is new shoes to continue my dance." Now the dance does not mean anything high, it means a kind of absorption in the ordinary world. He has become so accustomed to dancing in the tavern and has set his sights so low that when he's asked what he wants, he selects the thing that's going to give him only a momentary pleasure. In the Hasidic and Jewish mystical tradition, the worst thing that the evil impulse can do is make a man forget that he is the son of the king.

The challenge we face, even after years of religious striving, is to stay connected to the vision of unconditional love that awakened us to the spiritual journey, and to live it in a practical, meaningful way. Tempering the soul is a rite of passage in which we affirm this connection, not in words but by passing tests of our commitment. The tests may take many different forms and could show up as moral dilemmas, family or financial crises, or crises of faith. Though we can never predict in what form they will come, we know that sooner or later they will come. It is necessary that tests come, that's why tempering is an initiation.

The twentieth century Swiss philosopher Fritjof Schuon wrote: "Love is in the depths of man as water is in the depths of the earth, and man suffers from not being able to enjoy this infinity that he carries within himself and for which he is made. One must dig the soil of the soul, through layers of aridity and bitterness, to find love and to live it."

Spiritual aridity is the obstacle that tempering allows us to overcome when we have dried up or lost the intensity and the desperation. Bitterness is a layer that the sands of life heap upon us, pulling us so deeply into the world that we forget we are the sons and daughters of the king.

A few years ago I prayed for a healing for my father who was going in for heart surgery. I used every spiritual tool I ever learned and felt certain that God would protect and heal him. My prayers and visualizations did not bring about a healing, and my father died on the table. I went through all the stages of grieving that Elisabeth Kubler-Ross and others have identified, including anger towards God for not hearing my prayer. The only rock to which I could cling was my faith in the message of a religion that connects us to an eternal life, to a heavenly kingdom, and to the goodness, not capriciousness, of God. I knew the alternative is nihilism, a fatalistic existentialism, in which life ultimately has no meaning, no religio. I have seen too much and could never go back to that emptiness. But knowing all of this was not enough. I still had to go through a process, a passage beyond bitterness, to rediscover my vision, the unconditional love I was convinced existed in every moment. It was just hard to locate it at that time.

136

I made peace with God; what other choice is there once you accept that God is God? Eventually I came to the realization that in this instance my will and God's were not amalgamated, that I could not always get what I wanted even if I did everything right (as if doing everything right were even possible). I came face to face with my puniness, that insignificance at the extreme parameter of the I am created in the image and likeness of God but I am not God paradigm and paradox. Initiations are not always fun and joyous. They induce growth and so they are often sobering and painful, but they are also clarifying. It took a long walk in the woods to make my peace with God, a long purposeful walk, and my mantra was, "One must dig the soil of the soul, through layers of aridity and bitterness to find love and live it." Somehow I found my way out of the woods, and I understood in a more deeply profound fashion that though I am created in the image and likeness of God, and though I may be a mediator between heaven and earth, a channel for the light and energies of God to enter the world, that while all these things are true, still I am not God. And that was okay. It was but one of many temperings of my soul, but it was big one.

———————

Challah

One of the most prominent festival breads in our culture is challah, the braided Sabbath egg bread of Judaism. It is not only a beautifully symbolic loaf, with its three braids creating twelve sections representing the tribes of Israel, but is also strikingly beautiful to behold and delicious to eat. Like so many celebration breads, challah plays a role in the weekly sabbath, or Shabbat dinner, a time when family wisdom is passed from parent to child in a ritual that has been reenacted for thousands of years throughout the world. The key ingredient is egg, which probably is due to the need to use up the eggs before the twenty-four-hour no-work practice of the Shabbat. The dough is not difficult to make or to braid, but its role as a symbol of God's goodness and nourishment is yet another example of the centrality of bread in our lives.

Mise en Place

Makes I large loaf

4 *cups unbleached bread flour*

4 *tablespoons sugar*

I $^1/_4$ *teaspoon salt*

I *tablespoon instant yeast* (or I $^1/_4$ tablespoon active dry yeast dissolved in $^1/_4$ cup lukewarm water)

3 *tablespoons vegetable oil*

4 *large eggs* (at room temperature, slightly beaten)

$^1/_3$ cup milk or buttermilk

$^1/_2$ *cup water* (room temperature)
Poppy or sesame seeds for the top (optional)
1 *egg, well beaten* (for egg wash)

Mixing and Fermentation

Mix the dry ingredients together in a large bowl, then add in the wet ingredients, stirring with a large spoon until a coarse ball of dough is formed. If the dough seems stiff or dry add in more water. If it is too wet, adjust during the kneading. Turn the dough out onto a lightly floured counter or work surface and knead for approximately 10 minutes, adjusting the flour or water according to need. The dough should be very supple and lively, tacky but not sticky; it should pass the window-pane test (page 40). Place the dough in a lightly oiled bowl, cover with a damp cloth or plastic wrap, and allow it to ferment at room temperature for 1 hour. Punch the dough down (degas it), and knead it for another 3 minutes. Return it to the bowl and allow it to ferment for an additional 45 minutes.

Punching Down, Weighing, Rounding, Resting, and Shaping

Turn the dough out onto the counter and divide it into 3 equal pieces (approximately 11 ounces each). Roll each piece into a strand about 12 inches long. The strands should be thicker in the middle and tapered towards the end. All the strands should be the same length and similar in shape. If any of the strands resist extension, springing back to a shorter length, let it rest for 5 minutes so the gluten can relax and then continue rolling it out.

To braid, lay the strands side by side, about 1 inch apart, so that they are vertical as they face you. Beginning from the mid-point of the three strands, cross the left strand over the center strand. Then, working downward toward you, cross the right strand over the new center strand, and then left over the center, and right over the center, repeating to the end. Pinch the 3 ends together to seal and then flip the loaf completely over, so that the open ends are now facing downwards. Continue braiding as before, keeping the same pattern to the end, again pinching off the ends. Tuck both ends under the loaf to give it a finished look and place it on a sheet pan that has been covered with baking parchment.

Brush the loaf evenly with half the egg wash, slip the pan in a plastic trash bag, and proof the dough for about 60 to 90 minutes, or until doubled in size.

Baking, Cooling, and Eating or Storing

Preheat the oven to 325 degrees (300 degrees if convection). Brush the remaining egg wash on the loaf and sprinkle with the seeds, if using. Bake the loaf on the center shelf for approximately 1 hour, turning the pan 180 degrees after 30 minutes to bake evenly. The loaf will be a rich golden brown and sound hollow when thumped on the bottom. The internal temperature at the center must be at least 185 degrees, if you have a thermometer to check it, but if it sounds hollow and seems firm and springy to the touch, it is done. Allow the loaf to cool for at least 40 minutes before serving.

NOTE: Leftover challah makes fabulous French toast!

9

Living from the
Interior Priesthood

For sixteen years I assumed I was dead to the world but that was just practice. By that I mean when I joined the Holy Order of MANS I renounced all worldly possessions and as far as I was concerned I left the world to dedicate myself to serving God. That's why we called it a renunciate brotherhood. For me it was a formal, vowed renunciation of the world that lasted until 1990, when the path led back into the world. Officially that was the day Susan and I bought Brother Juniper's Bakery from the order and became the owners of real property, thus leaving the renunciate branch and moving into the lay branch of our brotherhood. The challenge then became how to be in the world but not of it; or how to be dead to the world, in terms of our vows, yet fully immersed in it.

Three years later we sold the bakery and bought our own home with the proceeds, completing the full break from a structured community life into a life of economic independence, leaving, as did other married members and families, the monasteries and the common life to the monks and nuns. Like all crossroads moments this presented both opportunity and challenge. It is not easy starting life over from outside the monastic gates with no pension and social security accrued, no savings, and very little in worldly experience. But living in a religious community for nearly twenty years did make us creative and resourceful. We knew how to create community around us, inviting our neighbors into our lives by doing the same things we did at our café, feeding them and inviting them to celebrate life with us. The first time we threw a neighborhood Christmas party, for instance, one of our neighbors commented that it was the first time in over five years that he had spoken with the neighbor on the other side of our house. It wasn't because there had been any bad blood but simply because they never saw each other.

142

Within a few years of living on our own we had figured out things like how to get credit cards, how easy it is to get into debt, and how many hidden costs there are to home ownership and independent living. But the biggest and most necessary challenge was and always will be maintaining a spiritual practice and living our values without the strong support structures and prayer patterns of our community. The outer death to the world signified by the years in the renunciate body now needed to be replaced by an internalized and personal surrender and a strategy for living that stayed consistent with the values we'd developed behind the monastery walls.

One question I was forced to face when we started our independent life was what are my values and convictions? It was easy when living in a community to be carried by the convictions of the community, but living out there on our own caused me to feel the full weight of my beliefs, my actions, and the underlying values that influenced my daily choices. It was like being handed a free will card that said, "You are now a spiritual adult, start acting like one."

There is a pivotal scene in the documentary movie, *Sunseed*, a film about the spiritual revolution of the '60s and '70s. Murshid Samuel Lewis, Sufi Sam as he was known in San Francisco, is surrounded by some of his young followers in a house in Marin County, just north of San Francisco, in the shadow of Mt. Tamalpais. Sufi Sam was a very charismatic father figure in the American Sufi movement, the first American who had been ordained to carry on the transmission of Hazrat Inyat Khan, one of the great Sufi masters of the twentieth century. Murshid Sam was the one responsible for the proliferation and interest in Sufi dancing, the ritualistic meditative group dance process that captivated so many young seekers. In the film his followers, living in a communal house, are grouchy and upset because the early magic seemed to be leaving their movement and they were getting on each other's nerves. They wondered if something was going wrong. Sam chastised them strongly for their lack of resolve, chiding them for thinking that the spiritual life was all about good feelings and peace and love. He called their whining "stinking thinking." Making breakfast, doing the dishes, living daily life, stepping on each other's toes—these are the realities of spiritual life. "You need to grow up," he told them.

143

Living on our own, back in the world, I often recalled that scene when dealing with my daily struggles. I was beginning to see what he meant. I had to prove myself and grow up in a whole new way. I was like dough that had been fermented once but now, cut from the bulk, needed to rise again.

A few chapters ago we examined the nature and importance of the primary fermentation in bread production. Now the secondary fermentation stage, called *proofing*, comes into play. Proofing is when the dough, having been shaped into individual loaves, must prove that it still has enough *push* in it to grow to the desired size. The yeast continues to feed on the available sugars, burping up carbon dioxide and secreting ethanol, pushing the dough into shape. It is at this stage that we find out whether or not the bread dough has, indeed, grown up and matured. If everything was done properly in the previous stages the dough should double in size and hold the appropriate shape. If the dough was handled too roughly in the shaping stage, or if the primary fermentation time was too short or otherwise inadequate, or if there just isn't enough leaven in the dough to get the job done, it all shows up during the proofing stage. On the other hand, if there is too much leaven in the dough, or the temperature is warmer than usual, the dough might proof too quickly, mushrooming over the sides of the pan or overrising and then deflating when it is transferred to the oven. It is entirely possible that the dough cannot sustain the rise, causing the gas to spill out rather than holding up the loaf.

Along these lines, the pastor at my church often concludes the liturgical mass by reminding his congregation: "Don't spill the grace." By this he means not to slip quickly back into worldliness and normal passions, to not deflate. Years ago I began viewing communion, or the Divine Liturgy of Holy Communion as it is called in Orthodoxy, as a therapeutic treatment for the soul, with the challenge being to carry this therapy into daily living. We may feel the peace that passes all understanding in the sanctity of a church service, or as a result of a deep meditation, but if we negate the remedy by engaging in activity or behavior that returns us to our unconnected, agitated, or anxious state, we "spill the grace."

We do tend to fall from grace almost as soon as we engage in life, regardless of how much we try to acquire virtue. There may be spiritual adepts and elders who have practiced a lifetime to embody the image and likeness of God, who seem to have achieved a state of peace and awareness not of this world, but even they are human and fall from grace in the course of daily activity. That is why they submit themselves to daily confession and surround themselves with some serious spiritual disciplines. Falling from grace just happens. Even when we strive as hard as we can for virtue the gravity of human existence naturally pulls us into itself and out of communion with the divine Source. This is the so-called fallen state that we enter the moment we experience ourselves as anything other than at-one with God; in other words, almost all the time.

Spiritual practice consists of both structured daily disciplines and applied opportunities to stay in the presence of God even while engaged in normal activities. This is the art of living between the rituals. It is the point in our lives where we are called to become priests unto ourselves and to sacramentalize every moment, which means celebrating each moment as a divine mystery.

In medicine, a homeopathic remedy is a microscopic dosage of a plant or animal cell that corresponds with our vital body, like unto like, triggering a healing response. Though homeopathy is still not accepted by the American Medical Association many people are successfully treated by homeopathic practitioners. Its history goes back through Dr. Samuel Hahnemann, considered the founder of "classical" homeopathy, to earlier days when the alchemist Paracelsus formulated theories utilizing symbolic language associated with the transmutation of lead into gold. Homeopathy, as a medical practice, is an applied theory based on this symbolic language as it appears in nature.

From my particular Christian perspective I have long believed that the ultimate homeopathic remedy is the wine and bread of a Communion mass. In this symbolic and alchemical ritual, transubstantiation, which is also called in some denominations transmutation or transformation, occurs. Bread and wine are changed, on some level (interpretations vary according to denomination), into the body and blood of Christ. In other words, to many Christians it is the virtual ingesting of God, or God's energy. As a memorial service, in the Protestant version, it is celebrated as a stimulation, a connecting through our memory to Christ and everything he represents, especially the message of resurrection. This is alchemy of a deeply sacred psychological nature, evoking whatever resonance exists within us, enlivening the intuition of our soul, connecting it to our outer self, and healing our souls of the distress of disconnection. In a sense, the priest's or minister's altar is a laboratory where the elements of spiritual science are brought together to create, symbolically, an environment for the possibility of communion with God. It is at this level that myth, faith, and logic converge, demanding a type of understanding that challenges us beyond reason. It is where we are asked to accept that metaphorical, poetic truth is as real as logical, observable facts. When the priest or minister invites us to celebrate communion we are being invited into a healing through celebration.

"What makes a celebration a celebration," the theologian Johannes Pinsk says, "Is that something other than daily life becomes accessible in it." In the Judeo-Christian mystical tradition, where every experience is a potential window into that other-ness of God, celebration serves as a powerful tool, perhaps the most powerful of all tools, a proactive prayer enacted on both the mental and physical planes.

The negation of the celebratory prescription is despair, signified by the popular bumper sticker, "Life is a bitch . . . and then you die." The word despair comes from the Latin root, *desperare*, meaning lack of hope. I have many times seen loved ones and associates, fresh from a satisfying worship, meditation, or even from a good counseling session, drift out of the ethereal realm of unbridled enthusiasm, determined to establish positive initiative, only to be derailed by a wave of desperare at the first obstacle. Spilling of the grace is not only common, it is the norm. Life is

hard. We live between the extremes of celebration and despair, between the rituals, wanting to celebrate but often finding ourselves
immersed in despair.

It was in the midst of grappling with this dilemma that I began
to connect the dots of my many life adventures, delving more
deeply into the realm of mediatorship. The Bible tells us that a key
to spiritual life is to pray without ceasing. Linking that to the ad-
monitions of the liturgists who celebrate the eucharist and remind
us not to spill the grace, I committed myself to extending that
spirituality into daily life. After all, a worship service at church or
synagogue, or even a spiritual pilgrimage, is not simply a filling
station where one goes for a refueling of spiritual initiative. It is
the hospital where one's soul can be healed and vivified to a state
of receptivity in which initiation and initiative become an ongoing reality. Formal worship is the microcosmic example of the
potential of our daily macrocosmic life. It is not a retreat from the
world, but a model of what our inner world can be on a daily basis as it expresses itself in the outer world.

Two other bread stages appear as parallels at this point, baking
and cooling. Baking is technically the application of heat to a
product to drive out moisture and bring about three chemical re-
actions. They are the caramelization of sugars (this shows up as
crust), the gelatinization of starches (the soft dough is transformed into firm bread), and the coagulation and roasting of pro-
teins (this is the skeleton network, the interior crumb or webbing).
When the internal temperature of the dough exceeds 120 degrees
the yeast begins to die. The living organism created by our hands
has given up its life while being changed into something other
than what it was. Raw, indigestible dough becomes delicious,
nourishing bread, the staff of life.

Cooling, though technically a distinct stage, is really an extension of baking as the bread continues to bake while it is cooling

down, evaporating off moisture, intensifying flavor, and more thoroughly gelatinizing the starches in what will ultimately become a cool creamy texture. I ask my students not to cut into their bread until it has cooled for at least twenty minutes, longer if possible, to allow it to continue its transformation. At this point, the bread has become what it is going to be; it is a finished loaf.

It takes little imagination to see the parallels in the human journey. Crucifixion, martyrdom, sacrificial actions, laying down one's life as witness, these are images that relate to this initiation. There may very well come a time in our lives when we find ourselves in such a literal life or death situation, but more likely are symbolic deaths in which our choices reveal our values.

When I was still a freshman in college, the summer just before my Highway 80 adventure, I worked with some high school friends on a demolition job in which we spent all day, for many days, splitting and salvaging beams and boards in an old warehouse. It was a tremendous physical work-out and each day we went home exhausted but feeling as good as if we'd been at the gym all day. We took turns driving and on one day it fell to a guy named Steve. Steve had always impressed me throughout high school as a person on an inward journey, someone always grappling with moral dilemmas and *who am I* questions, reading books by authors like Herman Hesse and Thomas Merton, though he never talked about it. He was a bit of a space cadet so it came as little surprise that we got stopped by the police on our way home from work because his license plate had expired. The policeman was a reasonable guy and when Steve explained to him that he did have the new registration only it was still at home, the officer seemed prone to believe him. But since he had his job to do he offered what I thought at the time was a pretty fair deal, saying, "I'll tell you what. I really should write you up for this even if you do have your registration at home. But, call me gullible, since I believe you, but why don't we do this:

The Policeman's Benevolence League is sponsoring a thrill show next week and I happen to have some tickets on me for it. How about if you buy a couple of tickets to the show and I'll give you a chance to replace your registration when you get home?"

The three of us crammed in the car, exhausted and anxious to get home, all offered to chip in for the thrill show tickets but Steve said, "I don't know. That kind of feels illegal or something."

The officer was a little flummoxed by that reply and said, "I don't think you heard me, son. I'm offering to let you off this time and am just asking you to help out for a worthy cause."

Steve said, "It just doesn't feel right. It seems wrong somehow. I don't think I can go along with it."

We groaned.

The policeman collected himself, amazed that his generous offer was being shunned, and said, "Well, then, I guess I'll just have to take you in and confiscate this car."

"Oh," said Steve, giving me hope he was reconsidering his options. But instead, after a few seconds of thinking it over said, "Gee, I just don't feel right about it, I'm sorry."

"Do you really want me to take you in?" the officer asked, still amazed at Steve's stubbornness.

"No, I don't want want you take me in, but if that's the only alternative, then I guess you'll have to."

Steve was clearly not being a wise guy here; there was no attitude behind his intractability. He was genuinely unable to compromise, and the policeman was totally unprepared for such a stand. He sputtered a little, then went silent. He looked at Steve, then at the rest of us who were pleading with Steve to take the offer, then looked at Steve again and smiled. "Go on, just get out of here. But God help you if you don't get that registration on your car."

We continued on home babbling like little kids about what had just happened. We all thought Steve was nuts to take such a stand but were thrilled to have had such an outcome. Steve had little to say except, "I just couldn't do it, it just seemed wrong."

I have since lost contact with Steve and have no idea how his life unfolded. He was a no-show at our recent thirtieth high school reunion, and we may never cross paths again. But that moral stand made a huge impression on me, planting a seed that became an integral part of my awakening. I don't know if and how his stand affected Steve, but I know how it changed me, causing me to examine my own integrity and values. It has been over thirty years since that encounter but the fact that I still draw upon the memory of it, and the lesson of it, reveals the impression it made and still makes. These are the kinds of crucifixions, or crossroads, that we encounter on an almost daily basis, the opportunities to discover what we really stand for.

The three bread stages of proofing, baking, and cooling parallel one umbrella initiation called *living from the interior priesthood.* This means stepping fully into spiritual adulthood and taking responsibility for the values at the core of our being, mediating between heaven and earth in a life dedicated to being a channel for God's grace to express itself in this world. In the mystical tradition this would equate with the rare experience of *deification,* another word for theosis, in which we are so infused with the energies of God that we experience what is called the *uncreated light of God.* In our times, and in most of our lives, the extent to which we can know this initiation in its fullest depends upon how we collect and string together our large and small epiphanies. Whatever brief moments of exposure to the unconditional love of God we have known become the inspirations that evoke from us a yearning for more. Then it becomes a matter of living from the interior reality these glimpses illumined, however briefly. It means being in the synergy dance, not waiting to be invited. We are all invited.

During the last scene in the film *The Chosen,* based on Chaim Potok's wonderful novel, the narrator tells the Talmudic version of what Christians call the Parable of the Prodigal Son. In this version the eldest son has left home and lives a debauched life but, at his father's beckoning, desires to come home. In his shame, however, he decides he cannot come home. So his father sends him a message, "Come home as far as you can and when you cannot come any further, I will come to meet you." That is how synergy, the key to the interior priesthood, works.

Confession is one of the ways by which a wayward soul returns home. Such an effort, almost always inadequate but always met by forgiveness, is synergy in its highest ritualistic and psychological expression. The process is a difficult one, sometimes made harder by its legislated aspect. Despite this obstacle some of the great historical confessors, such as Padre Pio of Italy or Fr. John of Kronstadt, who lived around the turn of the last century in Russia, were priests imbued with so much nonjudgmental love that thousands of people desired to confess to them daily. They demonstrated the efficacy of the confessional sacrament and the power of unconditional love, despite societal trends to the contrary.

In Eastern Christianity, a confessor need not be a priest but could also be some other spiritual confidant or friend. While only a priest is ordained to declare absolution, many priests will do so if they know a person has confessed to an agreed-upon spiritual friend. The important requirement is a spoken acknowledgment of sin to one who consciously serves as a living symbol and mediator for God.

The dynamic of confession is based on the principle of repentance and transformation, *metanoia,* an awareness that one's actions have caused a separation from God because they are not consistent with God's image and likeness. Confession is not the kind of therapeutic practice where one works out issues from the past. It is simply a declaration that the prodigal son or daughter would like to come home, to be received in unconditional love by the God who created us.

What helped me overcome my resistance to confession is the understanding that it is not the priest who absolves sin, it is God. While good counseling can often lead a person to a realization of errors, or to self-understanding, sacramental confession, on the other hand, results in absolution from those errors, or sins. It is not the priest who absolves, however, but God. Confession is merely witnessed by the priest. *Behold my child, Christ standeth here invisibly, and receiveth thy confession: wherefore, be not ashamed, neither be afraid and conceal thou nothing from me: but tell me, doubting not, all things which thou hast done; and so shalt thou have pardon from our Lord Jesus Christ. Lo, His holy image is before us, and I am but a witness, bearing testimony before Him of all things which thou dost say to me. But if thou shall conceal anything from me, thou shalt have the greater sin. Take heed, therefore, lest, having come to the physician, thou depart unhealed.*

The confessor is merely God's witness, a mediator who provides the vehicle for a spoken confession. Spoken-ness is a necessary and required aspect of the sacrament. While a private internal conversation may help to restore one's sense of relationship with God, it does not satisfy the requirements of the sacrament of confession. It is the act of confessing to a member of the human community that symbolizes the desire to repent in this world, at that point in time. It acknowledges the recognition of God's immanence as well as transcendence, especially as God manifests in the world and not just in ourselves. This is serious spiritual alchemy.

In Orthodox and Catholic churches one is not supposed to receive communion without having first confessed in preparation. When our order was nondenominational and nonsectarian we prided ourselves in serving communion to anyone, anywhere, even if they were not Christian, with or without confession. Our theory was that the taking of the Body and Blood of Christ would bring about a gradual transformation and, possibly, a conversion of the heart. By placing few restrictions on who could receive and by not requiring a prior confession we often served communion to large crowds of people. It became one of our trademarks.

I remember one Christmas eve when a group of Sufis, who were disciples of Murshid Samuel Lewis (the aforementioned Sufi Sam), came for Christmas mass. Samuel Lewis was actually an advisor to our order during its early years, until his death in 1971. Initially, the Order was very eclectic, drawing upon wisdom teachings from many religions, then weaving them into a Christian framework. The local Sufis who, like us, were young American converts, felt like our first cousins and were always welcomed at our services. It was customary for them to arrive en masse at the midnight Christmas service. One of the Sufi women, like me a Jewish convert, commented after the service that she really enjoyed it as ". . . there's nothing quite like a Holy Order of MANS communion." We were, in those post-flower-power days, very proud of our ecumenical and unconditional approach to the sacraments. It seemed like an important alternative to the restricted, rigid, and confessed-only version meted out at mainstream Catholic and Orthodox churches, or the memorial-only services in the Protestant denominations.

Later, when we converted to the Eastern Orthodox Church, we learned that communion could only be served to other Orthodox, and that they were each expected to make regular confession. This required a major adjustment in our thinking. While our priests had been trained in all the sacramental rituals, the restricted orientation was a new development. Some of our members felt this was a step backward, while others were relieved that we were tightening the ship. It was difficult for some priests who had been serving communion and taking confessions from anyone who so requested to suddenly switch gears and now insist upon Orthodox credentials. It required another change in context; we had moved from being a broad-gated, fairly liberal expression of mystical Christianity to the narrow-gated and conservatively strict form of traditional orthodoxy, with its mystical and ascetic theology. It was a trade-off made necessary by our gradually growing awareness that there was an existing historical expression of what we had come to on our own through trial and error. There were checks and balances in place and their main purpose was to protect the soul from going too fast, too soon. It was not as flashy as what we had, but it was surer and safer and fulfilled the same vision and goal.

For many of us, confession was the most difficult of the sacraments to look at anew. It had never before been a requirement to give a confession in order to receive communion in our movement. The sacrament was invoked mainly when someone felt so burdened by personal matters as to make it difficult to approach the altar to receive communion. Orthodoxy stresses the fallen-ness of the human state, along with the need for vigilant and constant repentance, while our order had focused on postforgiveness activity such as helping others. We emphasized the natural goodness of mankind, believed strongly in positive thinking and the power of personal prayer to affect change in the world, and the universality of Christian redemption, as well as the importance of service work. The change to a more introspective confrontation with one's tendency toward sinfulness represented a major shift from the founding principles that drew so many of us in the early days. We had been, initially, in revolt against what we called mainstream churchianity and all that it represented, especially its seeming ineffectiveness to make a qualitative difference in the spirituality of our culture.

We learned that there are two kind of confessions, *noetic* and *holy.* Noetic confession is the private internal conversation we have with God, the unfolding of self-knowledge that evokes compunction, defined by Saint John Climacus as "... an eternal torment of the conscience which brings about the cooling fire of the heart ..." (Ladder of Divine Ascent, step 7). Holy Confession, on the other hand, is the formal ritual in the presence of a confessor or trusted guide. Summoning the courage to reveal one's mind and soul to another human is a symbolic act of trust in the goodness and forgiveness of God. This is why the confessional is such a private and confidential ritual.

The essence of confession is contained in the Greek word, *metanoia*, meaning both repentance and transformation, literally, a change of mind. Confession is the ritual reenactment of the parable of the prodigal son, demonstrating the power of unconditional love to forgive and absolve a contrite heart. There cannot be, in a sacred psychology, transformation without repentance.

It is an enormous challenge for a priest to handle the responsibility of another's soul confessions. The confessor must truly understand the concept of mediatorship. If he or she gets in the way, attempting through personal persuasion to cause transformation in the confessee, not only does the alchemy break down but the confessor's own soul becomes endangered. He becomes like a clogged filter, and this can manifest in both physical and psychological illness. I have seen it happen, especially among ministers who attempted to provide counseling in the form of good advice. When their advice was not taken they were offended and became angry. In this regard trained therapists often possess more savvy in understanding the dynamics of the therapeutic alliance. From a sacramental perspective, to which the minister/priest always has to stay connected, any healing that occurs is brought about synergistically, not because of anything the minister says or does but through a renewing of relationship between the confessee and God. It is in reliance upon the unseen grace of God that the power of confession

155

is unleashed. The confessor's foremost responsibility is to maintain faith, not to give sage advice, even though advice may be forthcoming. It is to maintain transparency, understanding the importance and reality of the words offered up front in the "Exhortation to the Penitent": . . . I am but a witness, bearing testimony before Him of all things which thou dost say to me. . . .

What makes living from the interior priesthood an initiation is that there is a clear and noticeable distinction between the before and after person. It is a finding of one's true voice in which God-given power and authority comes forth naturally, not contrived. Most importantly, this power is borne with utmost humility and virtue, realizing that we are witnesses of grace, not the source of it. Growth doesn't stop, mistakes don't go away, but there is now such a totally new, transformed person present that the ups and downs of life, the events themselves, no longer determine who we are, nor threaten our sense of mission and purpose. In passing through this stage of the journey we now know who we are and how we are to be.

Bacterial Fermentation

There is a second kind of fermentation, rarely explained in cookbooks, that takes place in bread dough called bacterial fermentation. It is most evident in sourdough, or wild yeast breads. Regular commercially yeasted breads go through their twelve steps too quickly for bacterial fermentation to be a factor, but in wild yeast breads this kind of fermentation is encouraged and prized. Many of the artisan-style bakers pride themselves on their grasp of this part of the fermentation process. To some extent it is the final frontier of bread baking, like working without a safety net. It takes skill and practice to master wild yeast baking, but because of the more complex fermentation processes the results can be extraordinary.

A sourdough starter, so prized for its mysterious powers, is a dough in which wild yeast and particular types of lactobacillus and other bacteria have been purposefully cultivated. The wild yeast, known as *saccaramyces exiguus*, has one very important distinction from commercial bread yeast (called *saccaramyces cerevisiae*, the same strain used in most beer making). *S. exiguus* yeast thrives in acidic environments, while *s.cerevisiae* yeast does not. The by-products of yeast feeding on sugar are carbon dioxide and alcohol, but the by-product of bacteria feeding on sugar is acid, both lactic and acetic. Most bread lovers do not realize it, but it is bacteria that makes sourdough bread sour, not the wild yeast; the wild yeast merely tolerates the acidic conditions, continuing to do what it does best, ferment and leaven the dough. Commercial *s.cerevisiae* yeast would die in the 3.5 to 4.0 ph environment that *s.exiguus* yeast seems to love. When yeast dies it gives off another by-product, glutathiamine, an enzyme that destroys gluten and tastes like ammonia. Glutathiamine is bad for bread. For this reason you cannot make good sourdough bread with commercial yeast.

Sourdough bread uses its own preferment called, quite naturally, sourdough starter. In some countries, the starter may be called *barm*, *levain*, *desum*, or seed culture. Regardless of its name, the starter is loaded with both *s.exiguus* yeast and bacterial organisms, all living somewhat harmoniously, at least as long as they are properly nurtured and refreshed with fresh flour from time to time. The building of a world-class loaf of sourdough bread is a process of building small amounts of preferment into larger amounts until it is elaborated into a final dough, fermented again, and baked. This multibuild process allows the bacterial flavors to develop into a complexity that lingers on the palate hours after consumption. This long flavor finish is the final payoff for the added steps; it is what the mystique around sourdough bread is all about.

Armed with this knowledge, information I do not give to my students until they have shown a few weeks of competence with *s.cerevisiae*-leavened products, building new knowledge onto their old, the baker/students have, after five weeks, a full array of baking tools. If they practice and properly deploy their tools of knowledge, they can, in time, become decent bakers.

———————

Sourdough Starter

This will take 5 days, and the flavor of your starter will depend totally on the local bacteria and the bacteria already living in your flour.

Mise en Place

1 *cup whole wheat flour*
1 *cup raisins* (organic if possible)
1 *tablespoon honey*
9 *cups unbleached bread flour* (for all 5 days)
2 *cups water, lukewarm* (for the first day)
Water, at room temperature for the following 4 days (the amount will vary from day to day of the process)

Mixing and Fermentation

Day 1: Soak the raisins in the 2 cups of warm water for 5 minutes. Strain off the water and, saving it, set the raisins aside to eat or use in something else. In a small mixing bowl add 1 cup of the raisin water to 1 cup whole-wheat flour. Stir in 1 tablespoon honey and whisk the ingredients into a smooth batter. Cover with plastic wrap and allow to sit at room temperature for 24 hours.

Day 2: Add 1 cup bread flour and $3/4$ cup water (at room temperature) to the first-day mixture and whisk again until smooth. Use a larger bowl if necessary. The mixture will thicken slightly. Again, cover and allow to sit at room temperature for 24 hours. During this time the mixture will just begin to ferment, creating small bubbles.

Day 3: Add 2 cups unbleached bread flour and 1 $1/2$ cups water to the mixture, stirring again until smooth. Use a larger bowl if necessary. Again cover and allow the mixture to sit at room temperature for 24 hours. The pace of fermentation will begin to accelerate.

Day 4: The mixture should be bubbling noticeably as the fermentation progresses. Divide it in half and either give away one of the halves or discard it. To the remaining half, add 2 cups unbleached bread flour and 1 $1/2$ cups water, again stirring to a paste. Cover and allow to ferment at room temperature for about 4 hours, or until it becomes very active and bubbly. Immediately refrigerate overnight.

Day 5: Remove the starter from the refrigerator and, in a larger bowl if necessary, add 4 cups unbleached bread flour and 3 cups lukewarm water, stirring until smooth. (The lukewarm water is to counterbalance the refrigerated dough.) Cover and allow to ferment until very bubbly, about 4 hours. Refrigerate overnight. The starter is now ready to use for building Sourdough Bread (recipe page 160). It will have a fresh, apple cider-like aroma.

NOTE: To keep your sourdough starter alive indefinitely, continue to feed it once every 3 days, doubling the volume while keeping the flour/water ratio at 1 $1/2$ cups of water for every 2 cups flour. You may discard a portion of the starter so as to not need huge amounts of flour for the feeding. Exam-

159

ple: Pour out enough starter to leave approximately 4 cups. Add 4 cups flour and 3 cups water to double it in size. If you do not at least double the starter you will not be giving the existing organisms enough food to effectively multiply.

If you do not plan to use the starter for a while, you may freeze it for up to 6 months. Just remember to pull it out of the freezer in time to thaw (length of time will depend upon the size of your starter—but figure approximately 4 to 6 hours). After the starter has thawed, discard half and feed it again, according to the proportions described above, before using it.

160

Sourdough Bread

Once you have made a sourdough starter you can use it to build a loaf of bread. The most important thing to understand is that you are building a loaf in stages, creating an intermediate starter from your mother starter. This intermediate starter, called an elaboration or a build, is what the French call the *levain*, or leaven, for the final dough.

Mise en Place for the Intermediate or Firm Starter

1 *cup sourdough starter, room temperature* (take it out of the refrigerator at least 1 or 2 hours before making the firm starter)
1 *cup unbleached bread flour*
Water (as needed)

Mixing

Take the one cup of starter and mix it with the flour, and use just enough water to make a thick, *pâte fermentée*-like dough.

Knead just until it develops into a smooth dough that passes the window-pane test (page 40). Place this firm starter in a lightly oiled bowl, cover, and allow to ferment at room temperature for about 6 hours, or until nearly doubled in size. Refrigerate overnight. This firm starter is good for up to 3 days.

Mise en Place for Sourdough Bread

Firm starter (the entire piece)

4 *cups unbleached flour or high-gluten flour* (you may substitute $^1/_2$ cup whole wheat or rye flour for an equal amount of bread flour, for a more hearty loaf)

2 *teaspoons salt*

1 $^1/_2$ *cups water* (lukewarm to counterbalance the cold sourdough starter)

Mixing and Primary Fermentation

Break the firm starter into 6 pieces. Add the pieces to a bowl in which you have already mixed 4 cups high-gluten or bread flour, the salt, and the water. Mix until it forms a soft dough ball and then turn it out onto a lightly floured counter or work surface and knead for about 8 minutes, or until the dough is smooth and supple, tacky but not sticky. Add additional flour if it is too sticky. The dough should pass the window-pane test (page 40). Place the dough in a lightly oiled bowl, cover with a damp towel, cloth, or plastic wrap, and allow the dough to ferment for about 4 to 6 hours, or until doubled in size.

Punching Down, Weighing, Rounding, Resting, and Shaping

Divide the dough in half and gently shape each half into a torpedo shape, following the instructions on page 40, being careful to degas the dough as little as possible. You can then extend the loaves into either 12- or 18-inch lengths, or leave them as plump torpedo *bâtards.* Transfer the loaves to a sheet pan that has been lined with baking parchment and sprinkled with cornmeal or semolina flour. Mist the tops with pan spray, and place the pan in a plastic trash bag. Put the pan in the refrigerator overnight.

Eight hours before you plan to bake the loaves remove the pan from the refrigerator and allow the loaves to gradually wake up and proof to not quite double in size.

Baking

162

Preheat the oven to 500 degrees. While it is heating, place an empty sheet pan or cast-iron skillet with an ovenproof handle in the oven to also heat up (this pan can either be above or below the baking shelf), as well as a baking stone, if using. When you are ready to bake, score the loaves with a razor or sharp knife, cutting diagonal slashes about $1/2$ inch deep down the length of the loaf. Short loaves can be cut once or twice while longer *baguettes* can take up to 5 or 6 slashes. Mist the loaves with water and either place the sheet pan in the oven or slide the loaves, parchment and all, directly onto the baking stone. Pour 1 cup of hot water into the hot pan or skillet and close the oven door. After 1 minute, spray the oven with water, hitting the oven walls as well as the bread to create more steam. Wait 1 minute and repeat this one final time. Turn the oven down to 450 degrees and continue baking until the loaves attain a rich golden color. Turn off the oven and allow the bread to bake an additional 5 to 10 minutes, removing them only if they appear to be burning. *Push* them for flavor, extending the baking time to roast the grains as deeply as possible. The longer they bake, the crisper the crust will remain. You will observe a blistering of the crust that does not occur on same-day loaves. This adds a dramatic visual quality that many people like.

Cooling and Eating or Storing

Remove the loaves from the oven and place them on a cooling rack. Wait at least 30 thirty minutes before cutting into the bread, as it is still baking while cooling down. The sour flavor is masked when the bread is warm, but when the loaf is cool the full range of complexity will be noticeable. To store, allow the bread to completely cool and double wrap it in plastic wrap. Keep in a cool, dark place or freeze. If planning to eat the bread within a day, keep it in a paper bag to preserve some of the crackle in the crust.

10

Being in the World but Not of It

There is an eighteenth-century Hasidic story about a rabbi named Jacob Joseph: He was a stern and austere Orthodox leader in Szarygrod, bitterly opposed to the mystical Hasidic way taught by its founder, the Baal Shem Tov. At last, the Baal Shem touched his heart and he began to slowly change his thinking. However, one day he was sitting over a book in the Baal Shem's prayer room when a man entered and began to converse with him. "Where are you from?" the stranger asked.

"From Szarygrod," answered the rabbi.

"And what do you do for a living?" the man continued.

"I am the rav in the city," said Rabbi Jacob Joseph.

"And how do you make out?" the other went on. "Do you make a good living or are you strapped for money?"

The rav could no longer endure this empty talk. "You are keeping me from my studies," he said impatiently.

"If you fly into a temper you curtail God in making His living," said the visitor.

"I do not understand what you mean," said the rav.

"Well," the man said, "Everyone makes his living in the place God has appointed for him. But what is the livelihood of God? It is written: "And thou, Holy One, art enthroned upon praises of Israel," and that is God's living. If two Jews come together and one asks how the other makes his living, he answers, 'Praise be to God, I make my living thus and so,' and his praise is the living of God. But you, who do not talk to anyone, you who only want to study, are curtailing God's living."

Before the rav could reply the man was gone. He could no longer study so the rav shut the book and went to see the Baal Shem. "Well, rav of Szarygrod," he said smilingly, "Elijah got the best of you, after all, didn't he?"

As I've grown and passed through many adventures and life lessons one of the deepest and most enduring is the idea that God can appear any time in any circumstance, especially in the guise of another person. The possibility that God reaches us and we reach God through another is so profound that Mother Teresa built her entire ministry on this principle. There are also other ways to honor this principle, on both large and small scales, but the best place to start is wherever we are, in whatever we do. In the end, it is the way we best demonstrate just how far we have come on our initiatic journey. We have reached the point where we embody our deepest mystical experience, integrating and projecting our inner world in the outer world. The proof is in the pudding, as the saying goes, or perhaps for us, the leaven is in the loaf.

The final stage of bread production is called either storing or eating. Having authored a loaf through eleven previous stages, bringing to life a lump of inert dough by infusing it with leaven, presiding over its formation during the appropriate number of fermentation hours to develop flavor and character, degassing it when necessary to influence its growth, gently giving it shape while it has yet one final push left in it, and then baking it, effectively taking away the very life that the baker brought into being, it is now time to be nourished by that which we've created. There are few processes that are so clearly linked as bread is to the universal stories of creation, making it an obvious choice for the symbol of life, or of God's presence in the world.

The struggle and goal of the theostic quest is similar to this final stage of bread production. We too, from the perspective of the interior priesthood that is now the identity and nature from which we view our selves, attempt to function as the presence of God in this world, mediators between heaven and earth. To do it effectively requires that we be in the world but not of it; this is what we've been working towards.

167

Pita Bread

One of the most widely consumed world breads only recently became popular in this country. It is called *kobzi arabi* in the Middle East, *pideh* in Armenia, but we know it as pita pocket bread. The magic of this bread is how it puffs up in the oven, caused by natural yeast leavening and also from something called physical leavening. This is when gas trapped inside dough expands and forces the product to rise by the internal steam it generates in the hot oven. Croissants, popovers, puff pastry, and Danish pastry are popular examples of the power of physical leavening. In a pita bread, the dough heats so quickly that the small amount of gas created by yeast fermentation is able to balloon a thinly rolled piece of dough, pressing out against the top and bottom, creating a split in the middle. One of the important steps in the process is to rest the dough just before putting it in the oven, allowing the gluten protein to relax so that the dough puffs evenly. Relaxing a dough before shaping or baking it is key to the success of many products, such as pizza dough, *baguettes,* and flat breads. A good example is puff pastry dough, which relies totally on physical rather than yeast leavening to cause its rise. If the dough is not rested for thirty minutes before baking, it rises on a slant in the direction of the last roll-out. This is due to the gluten, which is tightened and pushed by a rolling pin and then requires time to relax and straighten itself.

Once the pita breads have begun to balloon, it is okay to open the oven door and watch with glee as the gas pocket gradually expands, forcing the dough to split. Kids love watching this process, entranced by the transformation taking place before their eyes.

Mise en Place

3 $^1/_2$ *cups unbleached bread flour or all-purpose flour* (you can substitute up to 1 $^1/_2$ cups whole-wheat flour for an equal amount of bread flour for chewier pitas)

1 $^1/_2$ *teaspoons salt* (2 $^1/_2$ teaspoons if using kosher salt)

$^1/_2$ *tablespoon instant yeast* (or $^3/_4$ tablespoon active dry yeast dissolved in $^1/_4$ cup warm water)

1 *tablespoon vegetable oil*

$^1/_2$ *cup buttermilk, plain yogurt, or low fat milk* (at room temperature)

$^3/_4$ *cup water* (at room temperature)

Mixing and Primary Fermentation

Mix the dry ingredients together in a large mixing bowl and then add the liquid ingredients, stirring with a large spoon until a ball of dough is formed. If the dough seems stiff or dry, add a little more water. Turn the dough out onto a lightly floured counter or work surface and knead for about 10 minutes, or until the dough is soft, pliable, tacky but not sticky. If the dough still seems stiff, add more water. If it seems too sticky add more flour. Place the ball of dough in a lightly oiled bowl, cover with a damp towel or plastic wrap, and allow to ferment at room temperature for approximately 90 minutes, or until doubled in size.

Turn the dough out onto the counter and divide into 6 equal pieces. Round the pieces into tight, smooth balls (pages 106–107, chapter 6), leave them on the counter, and cover with a damp towel or plastic wrap. Allow the balls of dough to relax for about 30 minutes. With a rolling pin, roll the pieces into round disks about $^1/_8$ inch thick and 6 to 8 inches in diameter. Leave the disks of dough on the counter, cover, and again allow the pieces to rest for 15 to 30 minutes.

169

Baking

Preheat the oven to 500 degrees, with a baking stone or an upside-down sheet pan placed on the middle shelf. Transfer the disks of dough onto the back of a sheet pan that has been sprinkled with cornmeal or semolina flour (or you can use a pizza peel). Slide the disks into the oven. (You may only be able to bake a few at a time, but they bake rather quickly.) After 2 minutes open the oven door. If you see the disks beginning to swell and pop, continue watching. If not, shut the door for another minute and then look again. If the pitas refuse to pop, allow them to finish baking and use as regular flat bread (sometimes a dough won't pop because it was rolled too thin, too thick, or too unevenly). Otherwise, when the dough pops, creating a balloon-like bread, count 30 and take them out (if you leave them in to brown they will be too crisp to use for pockets).

Cool the breads for at least 5 minutes before cutting them across the middle, making 2 pockets. Fill with your favorite fillings. Pitas are wonderful when filled with treats like gyros meats, falafel, hummus, and even avocado and alfalfa sprouts. Or simply use as a side bread to scoop up sauces and condiments.

One of the luxuries of teaching bread making, rather than producing it commercially, is that every loaf does not have to turn out perfectly. In fact, I tell my students not to worry too much about the outcome but to focus on the process. If the twelve steps are followed and you practice, the outcome will take care of itself. From the learning perspective a student grows more from his or her mistakes, but it is difficult for them to detach themselves so easily from their product.

I had one student who decided to make pita bread, one of the seemingly easier items on the competency checklist that each student is required to complete over the duration of the class. The problem was that I had not yet demonstrated pita, and I ask the students not to make items that I haven't yet covered. His pitas performed quite nicely in the oven, puffing up the way they are supposed to, splitting right across the middle and ballooning into an almost perfectly round shape like a softball. I usually instruct the students to pull their pitas out of the oven before they begin to brown because that indicates the sugars are beginning to caramelize and the dough is getting crisp. When this happens the bread will not flatten as it cools and it loses the flexibility that makes it so good for pocket sandwiches. The student, not knowing this, crisped his pitas so that when they came out of the oven they just sat there, puffed and far too crisp to flatten. They were useless except as croutons. I commented that as I watched him bake I was curious as to when he was going to remove them from the oven and he said, "You mean you knew I was overbaking them and didn't tell me?"

"That's right," I replied.

"Well, now they're useless. Why did you let me ruin them? You should have told me when to pull them out." He was actually quite upset, more than I would have expected.

I said, "Frankly, I'm not too upset that you crisped a few pitas. Look how much you learned; you'll probably never make that mistake again. Besides, whenever anyone gets ahead of my demonstrations they're on their own. You weren't even supposed to make pita bread today so I wasn't about to jump in and rescue you. In fact, I'm kind of glad you screwed up."

He really got mad then; I could see him heat up, his face getting red as his blood seemed to be on the actual verge of boiling. "What kind of teaching is that," he stammered. "My goal is to make world-class bread and now I haven't done it. I've made loser bread."

"So does that make you a loser?" I asked. I was enjoying where this was going. "Do you think the great bakers never screw up? Do you depend on your bread turning out perfectly in order to feel good about yourself? Listen, I let students make mistakes in this class all the time for two reasons. The first is that it's the best way to learn, so if you're going to make mistakes make them here instead of when you have customers depending on you. The second is that some of you hotshots don't really listen to what I'm teaching until you try doing it your way and blow it, and then you get a little humble and realize that I actually know more than you. So you do see what I'm saying here?"

He was still fuming, but now it was mostly from embarrassment. He sulked off and I was tempted to pursue him and keep the interaction going, which is what I would have done years before in

171

North Carolina with my teenage delinquents. This time, though, I knew a process had been initiated that required no further prodding. It would work itself out over time. In subtle ways, the student attempted several times over the course of the following weeks to tell me how I ought to teach the class. He challenged my methods and questioned whether I knew where I was leading the class. Rather than rise to the bait I finally said, "Look, the school pays me a lot of money to teach because they think I'm petty good at it. But I'm not perfect either, and I'm always looking for ways to improve my class and be more effective at delivering these skills to you, so be assured that I take your questions seriously. Do me a favor, when you finish the program and have a chance to look back upon your experience here, please tell me if you got what came here for and we can even talk about how I can improve my class. Until then, let me teach the way I know how and just do it my way for now. Later on you'll have an entire career to build on top of that and do it your way. Can you agree to that?"

He did and we got along very well from that point. By the time he finished the program (he had four other teachers after me in the various disciplines of cakes, pastries, fancy desserts, and chocolate and confections), he was one of the most focused and disciplined students we've ever had. On graduation day he received the Antoine Careme award for most outstanding student, and he richly deserved it. I asked him then if he was satisfied with his experience, if the program fulfilled his expectations, and if he still had suggestions for how I could improve my class. His response was, "I got everything I came here for and I think the program is just fine the way it is. Thank you." He is now a successful pastry chef at a large resort, where he also makes bread (something that very few pastry chefs do) and is embarked on a very promising career.

I learned something from my relationship with him as well. I really did mean it when I told him that I am always looking for ways to improve my performance as a teacher and to be as effective as possible in delivering the material and the skills. I actually implemented a few changes as a result of his upset, especially in developing more sensitivity to the importance the students attach to their product. Their bread does reflect them and their self-image, so even if I'm not attached to the outcome they may be. I made a personal commitment to stay sensitive to that, reminding myself not to project my own detachment on them, but rather to respect their need, that need being respect.

Every class I have and every student in those classes teaches me while I'm teaching them, whether they question my abilities or not. But I decided to take it a step beyond the niceties of such platitudes and, using the things I learned from my students, created a training program for myself and other faculty called The Transmission of Knowledge. In many ways it is, to this point in my life, the fullest convergence of the streams and paths I have walked during these past thirty interesting years since sticking my thumb out on Highway 80. It is my newest metaphorical extension of struan, the convergence bread of Scotland, the harvest of my many plantings as a communicator, educator, and, most importantly, an evoker.

The program is not like most teacher-training seminars that focus primarily on the structures of instruction, such as lesson plans, curriculum development, and segmenting a class properly for maximum retention. These are valuable and necessary considerations and the training covers them, but it first deals with the concept of transmission of knowledge, and establishing a philosophy of education. In our situation, in a culinary school, we have many instructors, each of whose primary career as a chef was working in some capacity in the restaurant or hospitality industry. They may have been taught in schools or they may have learned everything they know from working in the industry. The way they teach is based on how they learned. Instructors in all trade schools are usually former professionals in their trade who happen to now be teachers. This training program is designed to switch the mode of thinking from a chef who happens to teach to a teacher who happens to be a chef. It is a paradigm shift.

The most important part of this program is establishing a transmission of knowledge based on the philosophy of education that underlies it. I learned from my various prior careers, from being around teachers of many disciplines, from my youth work and the many times I failed to be effective usually due to lack of patience or another virtue, from my life in a formal religious community with a clearly established authority structure that became a crucible for testing my mettle, and from marriage, the greatest learning relationship of them all. What I learned is that the most effective way to transmit any knowledge, in this case culinary knowledge, is to be a role model. Our jobs are to be a link from the vault of culinary heritage to the present day. I called this philosophy of education, *the teacher as mentor and role model,* anchored in the idea that your actions speak so loudly they can't hear a word you're saying. In this philosophy the skill of the teacher derives from four talents or virtues: command of the material; command of temperament (including patience, calm under pressure, genuine caring for the well-being and success of our students); command of the finest teaching methods learned through training; and command of the mentor/model philosophy, through an ongoing relationship with a mentor of your own.

The final purpose of this training is to help each instructor identify and lock into his or her own unique teaching *voice.* This voice comes forth only when a teacher has full command of the virtues just described. It is a natural authority that requires not only being a great chef, but also being someone who really cares about the students. In surveys done with our students we found

174

that the things they wanted most from their instructors was command of the material, passion for the subject, an organized presentation, and most of all to know that the teacher was genuinely concerned for the student's success. When all four of these criteria are met the student evaluations of the class would go way up.

There is much more to this program, including a seminar training intensive, followed by an extensive period of one-on-one mentoring, but what most excites me is that it weaves together so many of the threads of my life. This weaving, while not the end of my journey, represents yet another significant milestone, a culmination, and another initiation. I have no idea how successful this program will ever become, as it is only in its formative stages as this book goes to press, hopefully to emerge sometime down the road as a replicable model for other educational institutions and even businesses.

175

More important though, it is the satisfaction of convergence, of a soul-satisfying integration of my various life experiences, that is reward in itself. I have found a way to integrate my understanding of the interior priesthood into my work, grounding it in a tangible service to the world while knowing all the time that its roots are not of this world.

One of the liberations of this fulfillment is that even though I would like to see my work succeed and be fruitful, I am not attached to that success. I have done my part in the synergy dance, my grunt work, the casting of my bread upon the waters, and now I wait to see how God will meet me, trusting that though I may not get what I want I will get what I need.

They say in the Christian tradition that every Sunday is a reenactment of the original resurrection Sunday, that every communion is a confirmation of the full range of sacramental initiations necessary to get to that resurrection. While resurrection itself is an end, it is also a beginning. Every rite of passage is also an awakening, connecting with the lineage of awakenings that have brought us to the present moment.

What I hoped to accomplish by writing this book was not only to tell a story about how I worked it out for me, how I connected the dots of my life into something meaningful and interesting. I wrote it to also say that everyone is interesting beyond imagining, born with a universal, priestly mission that has a corresponding earthly expression. In the depth of our being, at the level of our souls, we each possess a priestly dimension, hungry for a means of expression.

There are so many ways to access the mind of God, so many tools and windows into the fathomless depth of the mystical jour- ney, and an equal number of ways to describe the journey. Bread has been my guiding poetical image and thus the twelve stages of production make great sense to me as they correspond to initiatic signposts that I have given names of my own. In the land of narrow gates, of strong meat, the signposts have cultural and generic names, but I think it is a good idea to have a few personal names for them too. It adds another patina of character and complexity and makes them personally meaningful.

I know many people whose lives are and have been far more interesting than mine. What I had to do was decide that however it played out I was determined to find my life interesting because it takes being interested to become interesting. However, while there are many interesting people they are not always fulfilled people, on fire with a guiding passion that leads to meaningfulness as their lives unfold.

I believe the search for truth is connected to the search for meaning. Meaningfulness requires connectedness, and so, by degrees, our life dramas become a seeking for pure, meaningful connections. One of my teachers once told me that he defined purity as the full amalgamation of ourselves with our principles. This book has been about that journey, for myself and, perhaps, for you.

Total amalgamation is itself a concept that leads to endless contemplation. It is the metaphysician's and alchemist's goal. The fullness of the mystical vision is total absorption in the Uncreated Light of the Source of Being, until one becomes that light, that uncreated creation. If we are to believe what the elders before us have said we are all born to this destiny, even if we do not fulfill it till after death, even if we, because of our choices, do not fulfill it at all. Over the course of centuries spiritual elders have laid down ground rules designed to protect us from self-deceptive *prelest* and to eliminate the need for unnecessary trial and error, but we are like the hard-headed, self-determined Old Testament kinds of beings. We tend to appreciate only what we accomplish ourselves, in our own way. We suffer wounds but we also develop character. The result of all this individuality is a gradual appreciation of the wisdom of those who could have said, "I told you so." Mark Twain pointed out that as youngsters we think our parents are pretty ignorant, but then we are astonished at how much they learned while we were growing up.

Our weaving journeys sometimes take us to a point of understanding that there are both individual tributaries and also a few well-defined roads, or ways. Sooner or later some of us find our way to the Way, where we discover that much of what we figured out on our own is confirmed and much of what we thought we knew is not true at all, that it can be replaced by a more profound or evident truth. It is then that we choose to submit ourselves to the wisdom of the Way, however we perceive that Way to be. One crossroad we encounter, especially challenging for those who believe that more than one Way exists, is to submit to one and only one Way, even if we know that some of the rubrics and rules of that Way are contradicted by those of another. Each path has its own context, its own series of *religios* and bridges that lend reason and meaning to its patterns. Sometimes we submit because we understand and other times we understand because we submit. Saint Anselm, Archbishop of

Canterbury in the eleventh century, summed it up quite famously, *Credo ut intelligam*—I believe that I might know.

From the vantage point of one path, another path may look flawed, and vice versa. We sometimes forget that when we look out we see differently from when we look in, that our sight is influenced by the raw material of our context. What is important, though, is to stay the path till we find the Way.

I really only teach my students two things in the five weeks they are with me, and I teach this in the very first lecture, as I taught it in the first page of this book. Everything else I teach them is just an elaboration of these two things: Our job as bakers is to evoke from the grain its fullest potential of flavor. Then, when we have learned the techniques for how to do that, it is important to pick a bread and make it over and over until it is perfect, until every nuance of its potential has been evoked. Go deep, not just broad.

What I have called the theostic journey is a quest for meaning, anchored in connectedness to an unconditional state of being that is, by its very definition, unbounded by conditionality. It is a state called, for lack of a better word since there is no one word that properly describes it, mystical. It is also a state that, despite its unboundedness, has been well charted by elders who have gone before us. They have left us a trail of breadcrumbs that we may either follow or disregard.

In the forest of our journey, we must not forget the thing for which we are questing. It is not only to find a sacred psychology, for that is a gift that comes with the package, but to find a way of life that includes a sacred psychology, and that originates from a foundational experience, both archetypal and personal, anchored in unconditional love and forgiveness. We are striving to connect with a Creator God that has and gives meaning, and this meaning is called *love*. Phenomena, success, and personal power, seductive as they may be, provide little meaning without love. This is not an original thought, as any reader of religious teachings knows, but one that I earned in my own fashion, while searching for the way to the Way.

I have come to the conclusion that the way to the Way is to trust totally in God and follow deeply the path as it is proscribed for you, which includes the necessary confessions, submissions, and obediences that will inevitably be required. Regardless of our religious choice, it will, if it is a true Way, include a striving for virtue, an unseen warfare. It will stem from an experience, either our own or another's, that resonates intuitively within us, rooted in the mystical vision described by Moses, Jesus, Buddha, Mohammed, and others who polished this pearl of great price into methods and practices, into traditions and transmissions of knowledge. These strivings are all designed to take us on an adventure, through initiatic passages, and restore to us the understanding, the distant soul memory, that we can be in the world while being not of it.

179

A sacred psychology, in order for it to be both sacred and a psychology, must heal and also empower the soul. Religion, among its many functions, must be a "hospital for the soul." Of what is the soul healed? Of anything that prevents it from fulfilling its destiny as image and likeness of God, of *theosis*. That is what *prelest*, spiritual self-deception, really is—anything that prevents this fulfillment.

A modern saint named Maximos of Corinth consolidated much of what I learned during my thirty-year pilgrimage into a very concise statement: "Three things bring salvation to man: faith, works, and contemplation. For firstly, one believes from hearing; secondly, one does the commandments; and thirdly, one is granted union with God and enjoys with contemplative faith what he formerly believed with faith from hearing."

As part of my regular bread-baking classes, I also teach from a philosophy of global cuisine. The foundation of this philosophy is the interconnectedness of the four major culinary regions of the world, Asia, Europe, West Africa, and the Americas. Through the interweaving of these regional influences cuisine as we know it today has evolved. The art of cooking is a convergence of many influences that ultimately creates more and more interesting flavors. When a student or apprentice has mastered the specific regional influences, what might be called the primary colors of cooking, he or she is then able to connect the dots into a full palette of food colors that eventually find their way to our receptive taste palates.

This concept of a global culinary convergence reminds me very much of my personal struan metaphor, the harvest bread of western Scotland. As struan means the convergence of streams, we too are the result of convergence; it is what makes everyone of us interesting. I began my quest hoping to become an interesting person, but now I realize that I was and am, as we all are, each in our own unique and distinctive ways; we are all intrinsically interesting. As soon as we weave the threads of the various influences in our lives and find the connective pattern we become ripe for struan-like harvesting. This is especially evident in our spiritual journeys, for the ingredients are, and have always been present to fulfill Maximos's theostic formula. We just have to connect the dots and take what we already possess a step deeper.

A few years ago I was in Jerusalem with my family on my first Holy Land pilgrimage. One morning I decided to visit the Dome of the Rock, perhaps the single most important religious location in the world. This Islamic Mosque is also the place called Mount Moriah, where Abraham took Isaac to be sacrificed to God, thus passing his most important initiation in preparation for the Hebrew mission of Judaism. It is the location of the Temple of Solomon, the altar of the Holy of Holies, the most sacred spot in the entire Judeo-Christian tradition, for it is also where Jesus cast out the money lenders and declared his messianic mission. Centuries later Mohammed is reported to have ascended into heaven from the rock around which the now-gilded dome is built.

I entered the temple quietly, hoping to feel the special-ness of the place. The rock was protected by a fence that encircled it, allowing visitors to gaze down upon it. A few Moslems were kneeling in prayer on some beautiful rugs in the corridor surrounding the fence protecting the rock. I walked around the corridors, soaking in the thousands of years of converging history. Overcome with a sense of peacefulness I closed my eyes and prayed for world peace and unity. Unexpectedly, a security guard came up to me and said, "You cannot pray here, only Moslems may pray here."

Stunned, I said back, "Why not—same God."

He said, "Sorry, it is the rules of the management."

The entire situation had suddenly become surreal. I could not believe what I had just heard, so I chuckled. The security guard was not amused and asked, "So you will not pray anymore?"

"Yeah, okay," I answered, shaking my head in amazement while trying to wake up from what surely must have been a strange dream. I walked away from the guard and around the fence to another angle that looked down on the rock, wondering just exactly where the altar of the Holy of Holies might be. Without planning, I began to drift off in prayer again, surrendering to the peace emanating from this sacred space. Within seconds the guard was confronting me, buzzing like an angry hornet.

"I warned you not to pray. Now you must leave!"

"Huh, are you throwing me out of the Temple of God for praying?" I asked, incredulous.

"Yes, you must leave," he adamantly held.

It was the most singularly ironic moment in my life, and I knew it instantly. He escorted me to the exit and I found myself on the plaza outside the Dome of the Rock, the Mosque of Omar, the Temple of Solomon, and the Holy of Holies, in Jerusalem, the "City of Peace." I had actually been expelled for praying. In *Sacramental Magic in a Small Town Café*, a book I wrote a few years ago, I told this story and said, "Then I had an experience I will never forget. My body and mind filled with peace and, for just a quick moment, I saw that scene as if from an aerial view, maybe through the eyes of God (who could say?). I saw all of us, adults acting like children, squabbling over prayer rights to holy places, fighting over land rights to ancestral ground, and making war with other humans in the name of the God we all profess to love. We were all children, together, fighting in a big sandbox, and suddenly the whole situation seemed strangely comical. 'We will work it out one of these days,' I heard in my mind. 'Be patient. We're just kids.'"

We may never live to see the day when we can all worship God, the Source of All, The One, in the same way at the same place on earth. The meeting ground of that, as my Sufi friend told me, could only be found by penetrating our own religion to its mystical, traditional core. In the world we are still children in sandboxes, and it seems as if we all work for competing "management." But in our hearts we each desire the same meaningfulness, we each need the same fulfillment: a personal experience of the unconditionality of God's love.

We each have many goals and aspects of personal mission, many adventures that compose our concept of destiny, but my own journey has convinced me that there is one thing we all have in our common destiny, because we all come from a common source. It is the potential for the realization of mystical union with God—a union that is severed only by the greatest self-deception of all: that we are not connected, not in union. In our search for meaning, for a sacred psychology, for eternal epiphanies, the hospitals of the soul have but one goal—to reveal us to ourselves that we might know that there is but One and we are already one with It.

Afterword

The Blessing of the Struan

Each meal beneath my roof,
They will all be mixed together,
In name of God the Son,
    Who gave them growth.

Milk, and eggs, and butter,
The good produce of our own flock,
There shall be no dearth in our land,
    Nor in our dwelling.

In name of Michael of my love,
Who bequeathed to us the power,
With the blessing of the Lamb,
    And of His Mother.

Humble us at thy footstool,
Be thine own sanctuary around us,
Ward from us spectre, sprite, oppression,
    And preserve us.

Consecrate the produce of our land,
Bestow prosperity and peace,

In name of the Father the King,
  And of the three beloved apostles.

Dandelion, smooth garlic,
Foxglove, woad, and butterwort.
The three carle-doddies,
  And marigold.

I will put water on them all,
In precious name of the Son of God,
In name of Mary the generous,
  And of Patrick.

When we shall sit down,
To take our food,
I will sprinkle in the name of God
  On the children.

Notes

Chapter 3

44   The three Victor Frankl quotes come from *Man's Search for Meaning*, by Viktor E. Frankl, Washington Square Press, Inc., New York, NY, 1968.

Chapter 4

62   This is a term coined by Archimandrite Hierotheus Vlachos, an Eastern Orthodox bishop who has written a penetrating study on Christian healing called *Orthodox Psychotherapy*, published by Birth of the Theotokos Monastery, Levadia, Greece, 1994. His writings are theologically challenging, but I thank him for consolidating his ideas down to such a vibrant image, making accessible to laymen what would normally be the province only of scholars and theologians.

Chapter 5

69   Dante, Il Convito, II, 2–5 from "The Banquet of Dante Alighieri," translated by Katherine Hillard, Kegan Paul, Trench Publishers, London, 1989.

86   Nikitas Stithatos, *On the Practice of the Virtues, no. 13, The Philokalia*, vol. 4, compiled by St. Nikodemos of the Holy

Mountain and St. Makarios of Corinth (translated by G.E.H. Palmer, Philip Sherrard, and Kallistos Ware), 1995, p. 82.

87   *The Practice of the Presence of God*, F. H. Revell, New York & London, 1895, pp. 20 and 15.

Chapter 6

91   Excerpt from *The Press Democrat*, Saturday, October 8, 1994, Santa Rosa, CA, p. D4.

102   St. Hesychios the Priest, "On Watchfulness and Holiness," no. 132, from *The Philokalia* (trans. Palmer, Sherrard, and Ware), vol. I, Faber and Faber, London, 1979, p. 185.

Chapter 7

115   Archbishop Basil Krivocheine, *St. Symeon the New Theologian: In the Light of Christ*, St. Vladimir's Seminary Press, Crestwood, NY, 1986, pp. 22–23.

121   Karen Armstrong, *A History of God*, Alfred A. Knopf, New York, NY, 1994, p. 224.

Chapter 8

130   The Mystery of Salvation According to St. Maximus the Confessor. In Greek, taken from "Orthodox Psychotherapy" by Fr. Hierotheus Vlachos (trans. Esther Williams), p. 40, *Birth of the Theotokos Monastery*, Levadia, Greece, 1994, p. 122.

131   Nikitas Stithatos, "On the Practice of the Virtues," no. 23, *The Philokalia*, vol. 4, compiled by St. Nikodemos of the Holy Mountain and St. Makarios of Corinth (translated by G.E.H. Palmer, Philip Sherrard, and Kallistos Ware), 1995, pp. 84–85.

134   *Epiphany Journal*, fall 1984, p. 11.

135   Frithjof Shuon, from "Spiritual Perspectives and Human Facts (*Perspectives Spirituelle el Faits Humains*)," Faber and Faber Publishers, London, 1954, p. 283.

Chapter 9

146   Johannes Pinsk, *De sakramentale Welt*, 2nd edition (Freiberg i. Br., 1941) (discovered in a book by Josef Pieper, *In Tune With the World, A Theory of Festivity*, Franciscan Herald Press, Chicago, IL, 1963/1965, p. 6).

152   Traditional "Exhortation to the Penitent," from *Confession* by Metropolitan Anthony Krapovitsky (trans. Fr. Christopher Birchall), p. 106, Holy Trinity Monastery, Jordanville, NY, 1983.

Chapter 10

165–166   Jacob S. Minkin, *The Romance of Hasidism*, Wilshire Book Company, N. Hollywood, CA, 1971.

179   St. Maximos of Corinth, Modern Orthodox Saints, Vol. 2: *St. Macarios of Corinth* by Constantine Cavarnos, Institute for Byzantine and Modern Greek Studies, 115 Gilbert Road, Belmond, MA, 1972/1977, p. 78.